DAVID WHITWELL

PHILOSOPHY AND PERFORMANCE PRACTICE OF MUSIC DURING JACOBEAN ENGLAND

WHITWELL BOOKS

Philosophy and Performance Practice of Music during Jacobean England
Dr. David Whitwell

Copyright © 2015 David Whitwell
All rights reserved.
Published in the United States of America.
These essays were first published between 2000 and 2010.

Cover image: *Hatfield House,* from page 208 of volume 1 of *The County Seats of the Noblemen and Gentlemen of Great Britain and Ireland,* by Francis Orpen Morris. Public domain.

ISBN-13 9781936512850

Whitwell Publishing
Austin, TX 78701
WWW.WHITWELLPUBLISHING.COM

Contents

I	Music in Jacobean Society	9
1	Music at the Jacobean Court	11
2	Music in the Masque	19
3	Jacobean Church Music	27
4	Music in Jacobean Society	39
5	Music in the Jacobean Theater	53
6	Music in Jacobean Poetry	81
7	Music in Jacobean Prose	87
8	Entertainment Music in Baroque England	93
9	Military Music in the English Baroque	107
II	Jacobean Views on Music	117
10	Views by English Musicians of the Baroque	119
11	Contemporary Views on Performance Practice	135
12	Jacobean Philosophers on Music	149
13	North on Music	159

14 Bacon on Music	171
15 Milton on Music	183
Bibliography	197
About the Author	209
About the Editor	213

I want to express my appreciation for my colleague, Craig Dabelstein of Brisbane, Australia, for his contribution to this volume. His own musicianship, broad education and skill in editing is responsible for thus preserving my essays. Any reader who places value in having these essays in his library is in his debt.

Part I

Music in Jacobean Society

1
Music at the Jacobean Court

ONE IS INCLINED to feel sympathy for James I (1603–1625), the first of the Stuarts, for not only was it his unhappy destiny to follow the great Elizabeth I, but he was a poor physical specimen.[1] He was inclined toward books, young men and extravagance in dress. Among his many failings was a distinctly divine self-image, illustrated in a message to Parliament in 1609:

> ... for kings are not only God's lieutenants on earth, and sit upon God's throne, but even by God Himself are called gods.

This attitude contributed to the civil unrest and regicide which followed. His persecution of Puritans and Catholics led to the famous departure of the American colonists. Indeed, but for the departing American Pilgrims of 1620 and the 1611 English bible which bears his name, history would not even mention James I.

The coronation procession of James I in 1604 included a wide variety of court music, beginning with a fanfare by nine trumpets playing the "Danish March."[2] Along the procession route there was a kind of large arbor containing three ensembles:

> The whole frome of this somer banqueting house stood upon foure foote; the perpendicular stretching itself to forty-five. We might that day have called it the musicke roome, by reason of the change of tunes that danced around about it; for in one

[1] Christopher Hibbert, *Charles I* (New York: Harper), 17ff., quotes a contemporary description of a large body over weak, thin legs; eyes watery and too large; and, with a large tongue, over a small jaw, which caused him to make a distasteful splashing noise when drinking and to dribble gravy into his beard and wine down the side of his cup.

[2] J. S. Shedlock, *Coronation Music* (Royal Music Society, 28th Session).

place were heard a noyse of cornets,[3] in a second a consort, a third, which sat in sight, a set of viols ...[4]

At St. Paul's Church one heard a performance by the church choir with wind instruments.

... upon whose lower batlements an antheme was sung by the quiristers of the church, to the musicke of loud instruments.[5]

At Fleet Conduit a pageant, "Globe of the World," was given, featuring the allegorical figures of Envy, Justice, Fortitude and Temperance, each of which was represented by music. An eyewitness described the music of Justice:

It was super excellent Justice, as I take it, attired in beaten gold, holding a crown in her hand; guarded with shalmes and cornets, whose noise was such as if the Triumph had been endless.[6]

Here also was a singer accompanied by another wind band, "this song, which went foorth at the sound of hault-boyes, and other lowde instruments ..."[7]

James I maintained some forty instrumentalists at court, including a consort of six recorders, a consort of six flutes and a consort of nine oboes and trombones. Of course there were also players for ceremonial purposes, including sixteen trumpets, two "Dromplayers" and a "Phyfe."[8]

Although James I maintained a significant musical establishment, nothing about his court could inspire further aesthetic growth because his personal tastes extended little beyond entertainment. This is best seen in the accounts centering on the visit of the King Christian of Denmark in 1606.[9] An eyewitness describes the arrival, in part:

After whome followed his Majesties trumpeters, led by their serjeant in a cloake of carnation vervet, bearing the silver mace of his office, and the rest of the company to the number of 14 in their liverie coates, verrie rich and well mounted. Then followes the King of Denmarkes drume riding upon a horse, with two drums one on each side of the horse necke, whereon hee stroke two little mallets of wood, a thing verie admirable to the common sort, and much admired.

[3] "Noyse" was a synonym for wind band.

[4] John Nichols, *The Progresses of Queen Elizabeth* (London, 1805), III.

[5] In the seventeenth century "loud instruments" was another synonym for wind band.

[6] Gilbert Dugdale, *The Time Triumphant* (London, 1604).

[7] Quoted in Nichols, *The Progresses of Queen Elizabeth*.

[8] Thurston Dart, "The Repertory of the Royal Wind Music," *The Galpin Society Journal* (May, 1958), 75, and Walter Woodfill, *Musicians in English Society* (Princeton, 1953), 179, 296ff.

[9] Nichols, *The Progresses of Queen Elizabeth*, III.

> Then follow the Denmarke Kinges trumpeters, being 11 in all, decently attired after our English fashion, in cloakes of watched, guarded with blacke and striped white; blew velvet white hates, with bandes imbrodered with gold.[10]

[10] Henry Robart, quoted in Nichols, *The Progresses of Queen Elizabeth*.

In the principal entertainment, an allegorical arrival of the Queen of Sheba at the court of Solomon, the "queen of Sheba" was drunk and spilled a tray of goodies in the lap of the Danish king.

> ... overset her caskets into his Danish Majesties lap, and fell at his feet, tho I rather think it was in his face. Much was the hurry and confusion; clothes and napkins were at hand, to make all clean. His Majesty then got up and would dance with the "Queen of Sheba"; but he fell down and humbled himself before her ...
>
> The entertainment and show went forward, and most of the presenters went backward, or fell down; wine did so occupy their upper chambers.

Three other actresses, Faith, Hope and Charity were also drunk and,

> Hope did assay to speak, but wine rendered her endeavours so feeble that she withdrew ... Faith was then all alone, for I am certain she was not joined with good works, and left the court in a staggering condition; Charity came to the king's feet, and seemed to cover the multitude of sins her sisters had committed ... She then returned to Hope and Faith, who were both sick and spewing in the lower hall.[11]

[11] Robert Ashton, *James I* (London: Hutchinson), 242ff.

Sir John Harington, who was present for these celebrations, confirms the general climate.

> I came here a day or two before the Danish King came, and from the day he did come until this hour, I have been well nigh overwhelmed with carousal and sports of all kinds ... in such manner and such sorte, as well nigh persuaded me of Mohomets paradise. We had women, and indeed wine too, of such plenty, as would have astonished each sober beholder ... Those, whom I never could get to taste good liquor, now follow the fashion, and wallow in beastly delights. The ladies abandon their sobriety, and are seen to roll about in intoxication.

During the Reign of James I there were also some elaborate outdoor entertainments with appropriate music. An eyewitness describes such a scene during a visit to Althorpe in 1603.

> At that the whole wood and place resounded with the noise of cornets, horns and other hunting music, and a brace of choice deer put out, and as fortunately killed, as they were meant to be, even in the sight of her Majesty.[12]

As would be customary in monarchical society, we may assume the lesser lords imitated the taste and practice of the court of James. If they did not maintain a musical establishment, they could always hire musicians for special occasions—as when the Earl of Cumberland hired the York civic wind band to perform for a masque he gave in 1636.[13] Richard Brathwaite, in his *Some Rules and Orders for the Government of the House of an Earle* (1621) details the music required for special banquets.

> At great feasts, or in time of great strangers, when it is time for the Ewer to cover the table for the Earle; [the Trumpeter] ... is to sounde to give warning, and the drumme to play till the Ewer is readie to goe up with the service, and then to give place to the Musitians, who are to play ... upon Shagbutte, Cornetts, Shalmes, and other instruments going with winde. In meale times to play upon Violls, Violins, or other broken musicke.[14]

Braithwaite also gives us a glimpse of the highly organized use of music for travel.

> When the Earle is to ride a journey, [the trumpet] is early every morning to sound, to give warning, that the Officers may have time to make all things ready for breakfast, and the grooms of the stable to dress and feed the horses. When it is breakfast time, he is to make his second sounding: breakfast ended, and things in a readiness, he is to sound the third time, to call to horse. He is to ride foremost, both out and into any town, sounding his trumpet. Upon the way he may sound for pleasure. But if he see the day so spent that they are like to bring late to their lodging, he is to sound the "Tantara," to move them to hasten their pace.[15]

[12] Nichols, *The Progresses of Queen Elizabeth.*

[13] Woodfill, *Musicians in English Society*, 260.

[14] Quoted in Paul Jones, *The Household of a Tudor Nobleman* (Urbana, 1918), 175. This is one of the earliest references to violins in art music in England. The Diary of Anthony Wood maintains in 1658, in describing a violin virtuoso, that "nor any in England saw the like before." See Robert Donnington, *The Interpretation of Early Music* (New York, 1964), 535.

[15] Ibid., 229.

But since there was some danger that all this trumpet playing might frighten the horses, the trumpeter had an even earlier duty. In what was surely the lowest moment for the proud trumpeter, he had,

> ... to goe often into the Stable, to acquainte the horses with the sound of the trumpet, and the noise of the drumme.[16]

[16] Ibid.

Walls, in a book on Baroque music,[17] leaves the impression that the noble class in England in the seventeenth century modeled themselves after Castiglione, *The Courtier*, and were therefore practicing musicians. He points to William Cavendish, Duke of Newcastle, as one who indulged in poetry and music "the greater part of his time." We believe it is incorrect to leave the impression that Cavendish was typical of his class. There is considerably more evidence that in the latter part of the sixteenth century manners were changing and the English noble no longer considered the ability to actually perform music as appropriate to his status. The performance of music was being relegated to the servant class and this is stated again quite directly in James Cleland's *The Institution of a Young Nobleman* (1607).

[17] Peter Walls, "London, 1603–49," in *The Early Baroque Era* (Englewood Cliffs: Prentice Hall, 1994), 285.

> Delight not also to be in your own person a player upon instruments, especially upon such as commonly men get their living with.[18]

[18] (Oxford, 1607), V, xxv.

A contributing reason for this was an attitude that the noble should never be expected to exert himself to the degree required to achieve an expert level at any skill. This would certainly be required to be proficient as a performer of music, as Robert Dowland, in his *Varietie of Lute-lessons* of 1610 points out.

> Perfection in any skill cannot be attained unto without the waste of many years, much cost, and excessive labor and industry.[19]

[19] Quoted in Donnington, *The Interpretation of Early Music*, 118.

This attitude in no way prevented the noble from enjoying music as a listener. Roger North, in his various essays, frequently wrote of the tradition of private music in the great households during the early part of the sevententh century. In one passage, in particular, he recalls the music in the home of his grandfather, Lord North.

> He kept an organist in the house, which was seldom without a professional music master. And the servants of parade, such as gentlemen ushers, and the steward, and clerk of the kitchen also played; which with the young ladies my sisters singing, made a society of music, such as was well esteemed in those times. And the course of the family was to have solemn music three days in the week, and often every day, as masters supplied novelties for the entertainment of the old lord.[20]

[20] Quoted in John Wilson, *Roger North on Music* (London: Novello, 1959), 10.

Charles I was also weak in physique, and suffered from a speech impediment, but he was a much stronger personality than his father. Had he chosen as a model Elizabeth I he might have been a great king. But he followed the model of his father and lost the monarchy and was beheaded. After becoming king in 1625, after only four years he found so many of his subjects in opposition that he dissolved Parliament and ruled alone for eleven years. During this period when political lines were drawn between his followers (Cavaliers) and the Puritans (Roundheads), war broke out with the Scotch Presbyterians. Charles reconvened Parliament to raise funds, it refused and he dismissed it again. The next Parliament, called the Long Parliament, supported the Scottish position. Civil War followed and the new Parliament, entirely Puritan, beheaded Charles.

Charles combined his musical establishment with that of his father to create a body of some sixty-five musicians.[21] A surviving contract for one of them in 1640 reveals that they were exempt from some taxes, were free from arrest and another document records they were provided with both printed music and manuscript paper ("Italian musique cards").[22]

According to John Playford, writing in 1674, Charles was particularly interested in his private church music,

[21] For the funeral of James I, payments were made to twenty-one trumpets, twenty-one "Musicians for the windy Instruments," and thirteen "Musitions for Violins."

[22] London, Lord Chamberlains Accounts, Vol. 738, page 75, for January 10, 1629.

which with much zeal he would hear reverently performed, and often appointed the Service and anthems himself, being by his knowledge in music a competent judge therein.[23]

While there were some masques and other larger entertainments under Charles I, the accounts center mostly on the provision of musicians for meals.[24] Fortunately, the musicians were able to work out a rotation system so the same men did not have to play for every meal.[25]

Roger North recalls that during the period of the Civil War, during the reign of Charles I, music making flourished on a private basis, even though public productions were of necessity curtailed.

> Among other arts, music flourished, and exceedingly improved, for the King, being a virtuous prince, loved an entertainment so commendable as that was, and the Fantasia manner held through his reign, and during the troubles; and when most other good arts languished music held up her head, not at Court nor in profane Theaters, but in private society, for many chose rather to fiddle at home, than to go out and be knocked on the head abroad; and the entertainment was very much courted and made use of, not only in country but city families, in which many of the ladies were good consortiers; and in this state was music daily improving more or less till the time of the happy Restoration.[26]

After the death of Charles I, the Puritan extremists tried to create a democratic government, but it soon developed into a Protectorate under Cromwell. Religious toleration was established and Jews were readmitted after having been banished for centuries. After Cromwell's death anarchy returned and now even the Puritans were in disarray. After much dissension the public finally was willing for a return of the Stuarts.

[23] John Playford, *An Introduction to the Skill of Music* [1674] (Ridgewood: Gregg Press, 1966), preface.

[24] The meals themselves must have been rather amazing. Every year, at Whitehall Palace alone, Charles and his company consumed 3,000 carcasses of beef, 14,000 sheep and lambs, 24,000 birds, together with vast quantities of pigs, fish, boars and bacon. See Christopher Hibbert, *Charles I* (New York: Harper), 112.

[25] Henry Lafontaine, *The King's Music* (New York, 1973), 72ff.

[26] Quoted in Wilson, *Roger North on Music*, 294.

2
Music in the Masque

THE PRIMITIVE "MUMMINGS" of the Middle Ages, followed by the simple "disguisings" or "masks" of the period of Henry VIII developed finally into the highest form of court entertainment yet, the Jacobean masque. These were allegorical theater pieces, whose nature might be characterized by the titles of three of Ben Johnson's masques, *Masque of Beauty* (1607), *Pan's Anniversary* (1624) and *The Fortunate Isles* (1624). A typical masque usually began with a prologue in verse, with songs and changes of scenery, followed by a dance, actors, and then a main dance in which the maskers invited the royal spectators to dance with them. Instrumental music used in these productions was often played by one of the wind consorts, usually referred to as "loud music." A few examples are the *Masque of Queens* (1608), "In the heat of their dance, on the sudden was heard a sound of loud music, as if many instruments had made one blast," and in *Oberon* (1610), *Pan's Anniversary* (1624) and *The Fortunate Isles* (1624), all of which call for "loud music."

Sometimes it appears a more diverse ensemble was used. A masque given in 1610 at Tethys' Festival specified twelve lutes for four-part music, later "at the sound of a loud and fuller musique" and still later "the lowed musique soundes." The *Pleasure Reconciled to Virtue* calls for "wild music of cymbals, flutes and tabors." There also appears to have been a wider use of voices, as a later stage direction suggests.

Mercury called to Daedalus in this following speech, which was after repeated in song by two trebles, two tenors, a bass, and the whole chorus.

Percussion instruments are also found in the *Masque of Queens*, in which an "anti-masque" begins with a "loud instrument" overture and then the witches are introduced who play on "spindles, timbrels, rattles, or other veneficial instruments, making a confused noise." Another masque calls for instrumentation which reflects the diversity of the seventeenth century musicians. Another masque for which the full text and lyrics survive is Chapman's *The Maske of the Gentlemen of the two combin'd houses, or Inns of Court, the Middle-Temple, and Lincolns Inne.*[1] This work seems to have been performed by six instrumentalists, who first appear not as musicians at all, but disguised as priests. Later we read of music for six lutes, then six lutes and six voices. They changed to some unnamed instruments, for we next read "Other Musique, and voices." Still later, for a torch-light procession, the six musicians apparently played wind instruments, for they are described as "Loude Musick."

The *Masque of Beauty*, with music composed by Ferrabosco, began with a "Loud instrumental overture" performed by musicians seated in arbors, representing the ghosts of old poets, and attired like priests in habits of crimson and purple.[2]

The *Masque of Blackness* began with a song sung by a triton and two sea maids, accompanied by "loud music."

> Sound, sound aloud
> The welcome of the orient flood
> Into the west;
> Fair Niger, son to great Oceanus,
> Now honored thus,
> With all his beauteous race:
> Who, though but black in face,
> Yet are they bright,
> And full of life and light,
> To prove that beauty best

[1] See Allan Holaday, *The Plays of George Chapman; the Comedies* (Urbana: University of Illinois Press, 1970), 565ff.

[2] For additional information on the masques see Willa Evans, *Ben Jonson and Elizabethan Music* (New York, 1965); Edward Naylor, *Shakespeare and Music* (New York, 1965), 164; Gustave Reese, *Music in the Renaissance* (New York, 1959), 880ff; and Nichols, *The Progresses of King James The First* (London, 1828), I, 234, 346; II, 383; III, 124 and IV, 948, 988.

Which not the color but the feature
Assures unto the creature.

Similarly, the *Mercury Vindicated* (1614) began with a "loud Music" overture, followed by a scene in an alchemist's workshop. Here, Cyclope, tending the fire, sings to an accompaniment of cornetts:

Soft, subtile fire, thou soul of art,
Now do thy part
On weaker nature, that through age is lamed.
Take but thy time, now she is old,
And the sun her friend grown cold,
She will no more in strife with thee be named.

Two additional masques by Ben Jonson also began with a wind band overture, his *The Golden Age Restored* (1615) and the *Neptune's Triumph* (1623).

It appears that ensembles sometimes performed compositions between the scenes, or while the scenery was being changed. In the *Time Vindicated* and the *Masque of Queens* wind bands were specified for this purpose.

*At which the loud music sounded as before,
to give the masquers time of descending.*

Similarly it appears that instrumental music was performed while the actors change positions on stage. A stage note in Jonson's *Masque of Queens* reads, "At which the loud music sounded as before, to give the Masquers time of descending." In Jonson's *Time Vindicated* a stage note reads, "Here to a loud music, they march into their figure, and dance their Entry."

An eyewitness reports on the performance of a masque composed for "Lord Hayes," for his wedding in 1607, by Thomas Campion. We are told there were three separate ensembles placed around the hall, as if at the points of a triangle. They were a large ensemble of strings and keyboard instruments, a consort of "6 chapel voices and 6 cornetts ... in a place raised higher in respect of the piercing sound" of the cornets, and in a place shadowed by artificial trees, "those that played on the hautboys at the king's entrance into the hall."³

One "Chorus" was composed in such a way that all of these ensembles participated, separately, "in the manner of an echo." Later, during a procession, "the 6 cornetts and 6 chapel voices sung a solemn motet of 6 parts." Nichols gives the text for this motet as,

> With spotless mindes now mount we to the tree of single Chastitie.
> The roote is Temperance grounded deepe,
> Which the coldiew'ct earth doth steepe; Water it desires alone,
> Other drinke it thirsts for none.⁴

One of the most interesting eyewitness accounts we have of one of these performances is by the Venetian ambassador in London, Horatio Busino, describing a performance of Ben Johnson's *Pleasure Reconciled to Virtue*, performed January 6, 1618.⁵ He describes the hall and the ladies present in the audience, regarding whose clothes he found had "no folds so that any deformity, however monstrous, remains hidden." More interesting is his description of the king's entrance.

> On entering the house, the cornets and trumpets to the number of fifteen or twenty began to play very well a sort of recitative.

No one knows what kind of music this was, which substituted for the usual fanfares. Although Jonson also uses the term "Stylo recitative" in his *Of Lovers made Men* (1617), there is little extant information on English musical practice this early in the century to allow the obvious association with the new Italian movement we call opera.⁶

This masque, according to Busino, began with a "very chubby Bacchus" who sang in an undertone before the king, followed by another stout, drunken figure, "Bacchus's cupbearer." The first principal dance was by twelve figures dressed in barrels and wicker-baskets with an accompaniment of cornets and trumpets. Next came a gigantic man representing Hercules and twelve boys in the "guise of frogs," who danced and were then driven off by Hercules. A scene

---

³ *The Description of a Maske, presented before the kinges majestie at Whitehall . . .* (London, 1607).

⁴ Nichols, *The Progresses of King James the First*, II, 118. Thurston Dart, "The Repertory of the Royal Wind Music," *The Galpin Society Journal* (May, 1958), 74, suggests this motet may have been Ferrabosco 1's "Exaudi Deus," which is found in the wind band manuscript in GB-Cfm.

⁵ *Calendar of State Papers and Manuscripts existing in the Archives of Venice, 1617–1619*, 110ff.

⁶ See Gustave Reese, *Music in the Renaissance* (New York: Norton, 1959), 883.

change brought dawn at Mount Atlas, where high priests and goddesses "sang some jigs." Busino was not impressed.

> It is true that, spoiled as we are by the graceful and harmonious music of Italy, the composition did not strike us as very fine.

After a final dance by twelve masked cavaliers, richly dressed, following which the guests themselves, "each with his lady," danced the Spanish Dance. Apparently it was during this dance that the weight of the evening's hours and consumption had begun to slow things, for the king became angry and shouted aloud, "Why don't they dance? What did they make me come here for? Devil take you all, Dance!!" Whereupon,

> The Marquis of Buckingham, his Majesty's favourite, immediately sprang forward, cutting a score of lofty and very minute capers, with so much grace and agility that he not only appeased the ire of his angry lord, but rendered himself the admiration and delight of everybody.

Our ambassador, "half disgusted and weary," left for home at half-past two o'clock in the morning, after having been at court for eleven hours!

The typical masque ended with dancing and we are given the names of some specific dance titles in a large-scale entertainment project organized by John Marston, the "Entertainment of Alice, Dowager-countess of Derby," given for her arrival at Ashby.[7] When her Ladyship approached the park around the house "a full noise of cornets winded" and as she entered the park "treble cornets reported one to another, as giving warning of her Honor's nearer approach." As she entered the house "a consort softly played," while a speaker greeted her with poetry.

Within the house a masque was given, its songs alternating with consorts of oboes and cornets. In a typical song, we hear the allegorical character, Ariadne, sing,

> Music and gentle night,
> Beauty, youth's chief delight,

[7] Most of the text for the speakers and songs are quoted in A. H. Bullen, *The Works of John Marston* (London: Nimmo, 1887), III, 387ff.

Pleasures all full invite
Your due attendance to this glorious room;
Then, if you have or wit or virtue, come,
Oh, come! oh, come!

The first mention of string instruments is when the "violins played a new measure," to which the masquers danced. After some more songs, there were additional dances, "measures, galliards, corantos, and levaltos."[8]

Marston also wrote the text for the *Montebank's Masque*, given at court on February 16, 1618. In the course of this masque the characters provide brief tidbits of wisdom. Masculine reminds us that it was still not generally believed, Galileo and Copernicus notwithstanding, that the earth revolved around the sun, when he observes, "A Drunkard is a good philosopher; for he thinks that the world goes round." Feminine offers an observation which is not quite clear at a distance of nearly four hundred years.

> An English virgin sings sweeter here than at Brussels;
> For a voluntary is sweeter than a forced note.

The most interesting of these are given by the character, Neuter.

> Musicians cannot be but healthful;
> For they live by good air.
>
> Playhouses are more necessary in a well-governed Commonwealth than public schools;
> For men are better taught by example than precept.
>
> A Kennel of hounds is the best Consort;
> For they need no tuning from morning to night.[9]
>
> The Court makes better Scholars than the University;
> For where a King vouchsafes to be a teacher, every man blushes to be a non-proficient.

Among the numerous songs, we are attracted to one which is entitled "The Song and Dance Together."

> Lightly rise, and lightly fall you
> In the motion of your feet:

---

[8] The written text for Entertainments by Thomas Middleton are given in *The Works of Thomas Middleton* (New York: AMS Press, 1964), VII: *The Magnificent Entertainment for King James* (1603); *The Cities Love. An entertainment by water, at Chelsey and White-hall* (1616); *The Tryumphs of Honor and Industry* (1617); *The Triumphs of Love and Antiquity* (1619); *The Sun in Aries* (1621); *The Triumphs of Honor and Virtue* (1622); *The Triumphs of Integrity* (1623); *The Triumphs of Health and Prosperity* (1626). Also see *The Dramatic Works of Thomas Heywood* (New York: Russell & Russell, 1964), IV, *Londons Ius Honorarium, Londons Sinus Salutis,"* and *Londini Speculum*; V, *The Port of Piety* and *Londons Peaceable Estate*.

[9] Several passages in sixteenth century literature, including one by Shakespeare, suggest some nobles organized their hunting dogs as a consort, by the pitch of their bark.

Move not till our notes do call you;
Music makes the action sweet.
Music breathing blows the fire
Which Cupid's feeds with fuel ...

There were also internal masques within the Jacobean plays themselves.[10] One such example is found in Middleton's *Your Five Gallants* (V, ii). In this masque there is music played by cornetts, as well as a song which begins,

Sound lute, bandora gittern,
Viol, virginals, and cittern;
Voices spring, and lift aloud
Her name that makes the music proud!

In Marston's *The Malcontent* (V, iii) a masque is given, which is introduced by the appearance of Mercury "with loud music." The nobles who play the roles in this masque enter to music of cornetts, as expressed in the stage direction,

The song to the cornets, which playing, the mask enters ...

The dancing is also done to cornetts,

... then the cornets sound the measure, one change, and rest.

At the conclusion of the masque the stage direction reads,

Cornets sound the measure over again; which danced, they unmask.

When the duke is discovered, having removed his mask, the cornetts play a flourish.[11]

Thomas Dekker wrote a satire of an aristocratic masque, danced by devils in Hell. Of particular interest is his description of the masquers drum:

They had a *Drum*, after which they marched (two & two) & that was made of an old *Cauldron*, the head of it being covered with the skins of two flailed *Spanish Inquisitors,* and a hole (for vent) beaten out at the very bottom: the Drum-sticks were the shinbones of two *Dutch-Free-booters*: So that it sounded like a *Switzers Kettle-drum*.[12]

---

[10] Internal masques are also found in Beaumont and Fletcher's *The Maids Tragedy* (I, i); *The Mad Lover* (IV, i); *A Wife for a Moneth* (II, i); *The Coronation* (IV, I); *The Coxcomb* (I, i); *Women Pleased* (V, iii), an internal masque introduced by a stage direction reading, "Musick in divers places"; *The Queen of Corinth* (II, ii), an internal masque, for which the stage directions specify "singing and dancing to a horrid Musick;" *The Passionate Mad-man* (II, i). The "Masque of the Gentlemen" by Francis Beamont is printed in Beaumont and Fletcher, *Complete Plays* (Cambridge: University Press, 1912), X, 281; In Thomas Dekker's *Satiromastix* (V, ii); In George Chapman's *Byron's Tragedy* (II, i). See also Beaumont and Fletcher's *The False One* (III, iv), with Isis singing of "Songs, dances, Timbrels, drums" used in the worship of Nilus and laborers singing "To delight his streams let's sing ..."

[11] The written text for masques by Thomas Middleton are given in *The Works of Thomas Middleton* (New York: AMS Press, 1964), VII: *The World tost at Tennis* (1620), which includes stage directions for "Music striking up a light fantastic air" and "Loud music sounding," for Jupiter; *The Inner-Temple Masque* (1619); the masque *The Triumphs of Truth* with *The Entertainment at the Opening of the New River* (1613).

[12] Thomas Dekker, *The Catch-Pols Masque* (1609), in Grosart, *The Non-Dramatic Works of Thomas Dekker* (New York: Russell & Russell, 1963), III, 365. Thomas Dekker (b. 1570) was a very fluent writer, producing plays of his own and in collaboration with others, in addition to "entertainments" and pamphlets on a variety of subjects. It has been said that no writer gave a more vivid picture of London at this time. He, however, failed to earn a living and was often in prison—once for three years. Nothing is known of him after the 1630s.

Finally, we must point out that Francis Bacon (1561–1626), who has been called "the greatest and proudest intellect of the age,"[13] wrote an essay, "Of Masques and Triumphs." In this essay he apologizes for including this subject among his other essays, he adds that masques and triumphs "are but toys, to come amongst serious observations." Nevertheless, he cannot hide his enjoyment of them.

[13] Will Durant, *The Age of Reason Begins* (New York: Simon and Schuster, 1961), 169, 183.

> Dancing to song is a thing of great state and pleasure. I understand it, that the song be in choir, placed aloft, and accompanied with some broken music; and then the verse be fitted to the device. Acting in song, especially in dialogues, has an extreme good grace; I say acting, not dancing (for that is a mean and vulgar thing); and the voices of the dialogue would be strong and manly (a bass and a tenor; no treble); and the verse high and tragical; not nice or dainty. Several choirs, placed one over against another, and taking the voice by catches, anthem-wise, give great pleasure.[14]

[14] "Of Masques and Triumphs," in *The Works of Francis Bacon*, ed. James Spedding (Cambridge: Cambridge University Press, 1869), XII, 209ff.

Among the specific recommendations for the music of masques, Bacon suggests,

> Let the songs be loud and cheerful, and not chirpings or pulings. Let the music likewise be sharp and loud, and well placed ...
> Let anti-masques not be long; they have been commonly of fools, satyrs, baboons, wild-men, antics, beasts, sprites, witches ... Let the music of them be recreative, and with some strange changes.

3
Jacobean Church Music

FOR THE FIRST HALF of the seventeenth century the instrumental music heard in the important churches in England consisted of the organ and wind instruments. Strings begin to appear during the Restoration, but the real story is the efforts of the Puritans to ban all instrumental music from the church. They succeeded to the point of destroying all church organs in England!

For the Jacobean and Cromwell Periods there were still some large scale church performances accompanied by wind instruments, as we read in an account of King James' visit to St. Paul's Cathedral in 1620.

> ... they began to celebrate Divine Service, which was solemnly performed with organs, cornets, and sagbots.[1]

In the king's Chapel, such performances appear to have been a regular occurrence, as suggested by a pay account for twelve wind players in 1633 under the title,

> Order to be observed throughout the year by his Majesty's musitions for the wind instruments for waiting in the Chappell.[2]

The major cathedrals of England, including York, Norwich, Exeter, Winchester, Worchester, Salisbury, Durham and Lincoln, followed this practice[3] and some churches, such as the Chapel Royal in Scotland, actually imported wind players

[1] Quoted in John Nichols, *The Progresses of King James the First* (London, 1828), 601.

[2] Quoted in Henry Lafontaine, *The King's Music* (New York, 1973), 87. One observer suggests that the winds were located in performance "in the middle of the Choristers." See *The Autobiographical Notes of Elias Ashmole*, ed. C. H. Josten (Oxford, 1966), IV, 1380.

[3] Andrew Parrott, "Grett and Solompne Singing," *Early Music* 6, no. 2 (April, 1978): 184; and Walter Woodfill, *Musicians in English Society* (Princeton, 1953), 149.

from London for this purpose. One Edward Kellie, Master of the Chapel Royal in Scotland, for example, came to London in 1632 and,

> Carried home an organist and two men for playing on cornets and sackbuts ... most exquisite in their severall faculties.[4]

Parrott found only one reference for this entire period which even mentions string instruments in the church.[5] Aside from the fact that it was the wind instrumentalists who had for so long been regarded as the *professional* musicians, at least one observer concluded that strings simply could not play in tune as well as winds. String instruments, he noted,

> ar often out of tun; (Which soomtime happeneth in the mids of the Musik, when it is neither good to continue, nor to correct the fault) therefore, to avoid all offence (where the least shoolde not bee given) in our Chyrch-solemnities only the Winde-instruments (whose Notes ar constant) bee in use.[6]

Before considering the impact of the Puritans, we should pause to read some of the references to church music which are found in the Jacobean plays, since from the generation before Shakespeare it had been one aim of the stage works to present daily life accurately, as seen in a mirror as some said. To begin with, curiously one finds a number of references to incidental music used in cult religious services.[7] Jonson's tragedy *Sejanus* (V, lines 170ff), written in the style of an ancient Roman play, includes a simulated ancient religious sacrifice, in which the stage direction calls for the ancient *Tubicines* (trumpets) and *Tibicines* (aulai) to sound as the priest prepares for the ceremony.

There are two cult ceremonies with music mentioned in the plays of Beaumont and Fletcher. First, in *The Knight of Malta* (II, v) the stage directions call for a Flourish, to announce the beginning of a cult religious rite.

> And so let's march to the Temple, sound those Instruments,
> That were the signal to a day of blood;
> Evil beginning hours may end in good.

Later in this same play (V, ii) the stage direction describes music for another service.

[4] W. Dauney, *Ancient Scottish Melodies* (Edinburgh, 1838), 365.

[5] Parrott, "Grett and Solompne Singing," 186.

[6] Charles Butler, *Principles of Musick* (1636), quoted in Parrott, Ibid.

[7] See also Beaumont and Fletcher's *Bonduca* (III, i), for music for a Druid sacrifice, and Dekker's *The Virgin Martyr* (III, ii), for music for a pagan service in worship of an "Image of great Jupiter," and *The Sun's-Darling* begins with a song at the altar to the worship of the Sun.

> *Musick.*
> *An Alter discovered, with Tapers, and a Book on it.*
> *The two Bishops stand on each side of it; Mountferrat,*
> *as the Song is singing, ascends up the Altar.*

In *The Two Noble Kinsmen* (V, i) a rather detailed religious service begins with Thesius,

> Now let 'em enter, and before the gods
> Tender their holy Prayers: . . .

This is immediately followed by a "Flourish of Cornets." Later "Musick" is heard while doves are released. After the ritual of bowing to the goddess, the stage direction calls for "Still Musick of Recorders." At the end of the service, a mechanical tree appears, bearing a single rose. The stage direction now reads,

> *Here is heard a sodain twang of Instruments,*
> *and the Rose falls from the Tree.*

A reference to music in a traditional religious service can be seen in Jonson's comedy *The Alchemist* (III, ii), where Subtle is criticizing a pastor from Amsterdam, Tribulation Wholesome, and makes this reference to church music.[8]

> SUBTLE. And get a tune, to call the flock together:
>   For (to say sooth) a tune does much with women,
>   And other phlegmatic people; it is your bell.
> ANANIAS. Bells are profane: a tune may be religious.

In Webster's *The Dutchesse of Malfy* (III, iv), there is a ceremony for the installation of Cardinals, for which the stage direction reads,

> *During all which Ceremony, this Verse is sung*
> *(to very sollemne Musique) by divers Church-men.*

And in Beaumont and Fletcher's *The Pilgrim* (V, vi) an extended service at an altar with stage directions also calling for "Solemn Musick" throughout. There is also an interesting reference to a funeral service at the conclusion of Beaumont and Fletcher's *Cupid's Revenge* (V, i), where Age commands,

[8] See also Beaumont and Fletcher's *The Pilgrim* (V, vi), for an extended service at an altar with stage directions calling for "Solemn Musick" throughout, and a service accompanied by recorders in John Ford's, *The Broken Heart* (V, iii).

> Go, and let the Trumpets sound
> Some mournful thing, whilst we convey the body
> Of this unhappy Prince unto the Court . . .

The great crisis in English church music came with the civil war and the Cromwell Period, brought about by the views of the Puritans. The Puritans wanted a return to the simple, unaccompanied psalms of the early Christians and in the prefaces of their song books we can see their belief in the moral value of such music.

> Set forth and allowed to be sung in all churches, of all the people before and after sermons: and moreover in private houses, for their godly solace and comfort, laying apart all ungodly songs and ballads, which tend only to the nourishing of vice, and the corrupting of youth.[9]

The stream of opinion which allowed the Puritans to prevail had actually begun much earlier, particularly with respect to the organ. The organ had come under attack during the reign of Edward VI[10] and during the reign of Elizabeth survived a motion for abolition by a single vote.[11] As an aftermath of the civil war, during the 1640s many cathedral organs were damaged. An account from Exeter, for example, records that soldiers,

> brake down the organs, and taking two or three hundred pipes with them in a most scorneful and contemptuous manner, went up and down the streets piping with them; and meeting with some of the Choristers of the Church, whose surplices they had stolne before, and imployed them to base servile offices, scoffingly told them, "Boyes, we have spoyled your trade, you most goe and sing hot pudding pyes."[12]

One of the objections to instrumental music in the church by the Puritans was that they obscured the words of the singers, the words being held more important than the music.

> . . . though it is not in Latin, yet by reason of the confusedness of voices of so many singers, with a multitude of melodious instruments . . . the greatest part of the service is no better understood, then if it weare in Hebrue or Irish.[13]

---

[9] Sternhold and Hopkins, *Whole Book of Psalms*, quoted in Peter Walls, "London, 1603–49," in *The Early Baroque Era* (Englewood Cliffs: Prentice Hall, 1994), 295.

[10] H. Davey, *History of English Music* (London, 1921), 107. A Church document of this period lists the organ as one of "84 Faults and Abuses of Religion."

[11] J. Strype, *Annals of the Reformation* (London, 1709), 298–299.

[12] Peter Holman, in "London: Commonwealth and Restoration," in *The Early Baroque Era*, 307.

[13] G. Ornsby, ed., "The Correspondence of John Cosin, D.D.," in *Surtee Society* (London, 1869), LII, 166.

One preacher in Durham, Peter Smart in 1630, argued that even singing was inappropriate to the purpose of the service.

> Our Durhamers have been so eager upon piping and singing, that instead of the Morning Prayer at 6 of the clock, which was wont to be read distinctly and plainly, for Schoolers, and Artificers before they began their work, they brought in a solemne Service, with singing and Organs, Sackbuts and Cornets, little whereof could be understood of the people, neither would they suffer the Sacrament to be administered without a continuall noise of Musick, both instrumentall and vocal, to the great disturbance of these holy actions.[14]

[14] Peter Smart, *A Catalogue of Superstitious Innovations* (London, 1642), 9.

This view followed the fact that the Puritans wished to remove from the service all the elaborate trappings of the old Catholic tradition. The view, according to this same preacher in a sermon of 1628, was that these, including music, distracted the worshiper.

> This makes me call to remembrance, a strange speech little better than blasphemy, uttered lately by a young man, in the presence of his Lord, and many learned men: "I had rather goe forty miles to a good service, then two miles to a Sermon." And what meant he by a good service? His meaning was manifest; where goodly Babylonish robes were worn, imbroydered with images. Where he might heare a delicate noise of singers, with Shakebuts, and Cornets, and Organs, and if it were possible, all kinde of Musicke, used at the dedication of Nabuchodonosors golden Image ... For if religion consist in Altar-ducking, Cope-wearing, Organ-playing, piping and singing ... If I say religion consist in these and such like superstitious vanities, ceremoniall fooleries, apish toyes, and popish trinckets, we had never more Religion then now.[15]

[15] Peter Smart, *A Sermon Preached in the Cathedrall Church of Durham, July 7, 1628* (London, 1640), 22ff.

The following year, in a publication called, *A Short Treatise of Altars, Altar-furniture, Altar-cringing and Musick of all the Quire, singing-men and Choristers,* Smart was even more vigorous in his view.

> Why then are set before us so many objects of vanity, so many allurements of our outward senses, our eyes & eares, & consequently our minds from the meditation of Christs death & passion, and our sins which were the only cause of all our miseries & his lamentable sufferings. Can such paltry

toyes being to our memory Christ and his blood-shedding? Crosses, Crucifixes, Tapers, Candlesticks, gilded angels, sumptuous Organs, with Sackbuts & Cornets piping so loud at the Communion table, that they may be heard halfe a mile from the Church? No ... Such glorious spectacles, draw away from God the minds of them that pray, they further not, but hinder entire affections, and godly meditations.[16]

[16] Smart, *A Catalogue*, 19.

There were some voices heard who argued in favor of instrumental music in the church and they made the basis of their argument the Old Testament. One example reads,

Wherein doth our practice of singing and playing with instruments in his Majesty's chapel and our cathedral churches differ from the practice of David, the priests and Levites? Do we not make one sign in praising and thanking God with voices and instruments of all sorts?[17]

[17] H. Peacham, *The Compleat Gentleman* (1622).

Another who made this connection was the philosopher, John Donne (1572–1631):

In the first institution of thy Church, in this world, in the foundation of thy Militant Church, among the Jews, thou didst appoint the calling of the assembly in, to be by Trumpet, and when they were in, then thou gave them the sound of bells, in the garment of the priest. In the Triumphant Church, thou employs both too, but in an inverted order; we enter into the Triumphant Church by the sound of bells ... and then we receive our further edification, or consummation, by the sound of Trumpets, at the Resurrection. The sound of thy Trumpets thou didst impart to secular and civil uses too, but the sound of bells only to sacred.[18]

[18] John Donne, *Devotions Upon Emergent Occasion*, ed. Anthony Raspa (Montreal: McGill-Queen's University Press, 1975), 83.

The power of the language in the Old Testament which praises the use of instrumental music in the service must have been a strong obstacle for the Puritans who wanted to abolish instrumental music altogether. And some, like the famous John Milton (1608–1674), who was otherwise a Puritan, appears to have been inclined to keep music in the service but seems to have wanted to define its character and use it carefully. Music, he says, should be a,

power beside the office of a pulpit, to inbreed and cherish in a great people the seeds of virtue, and public civility, to allay the perturbations of the mind, and set the affections in right tune, to celebrate in glorious and lofty Hymns the throne and equipage of Gods Almightinesse, and what he works, and what he suffers to be wrought with high providence in his Church, to sing the victorious agonies of Martyrs and Saints, the deeds and triumphs of just and pious Nations ...[19]

This might be an appropriate place to pause and read some of Milton's comments on church music in his poetry. First, like all early Christian writers, Milton is disrespectful toward the music of the "pagans," which is to say the ancient Greeks.

[19] "Church-Government," in *The Works of John Milton,* ed. Frank Patterson (New York: Columbia University Press, 1931-1938), III, 238.

> While they loudest sing
> The vices of their Deities, and their own
> In Fable, Hymn, or Song, so personating
> Their Gods ridiculous, and themselves past shame.
> Remove their swelling Epithets thick laid
> As varnish on a Harlots cheek, the rest,
> Thin sown with aught of profit or delight,
> Will far be found unworthy to compare
> With *Sion's* songs, to all true tastes excelling,
> Where God is praised aright ...[20]

[20] "Paradise Regained," IV, 339, in Ibid., II, 471.

On more contemporary religious themes, Milton devotes one entire poem, "At a solemn Musick," to the use of music as a metaphorical expression of the joy of religious life.

> Blest pair of Sirens, pledges of Heaven's joy,
> Sphere-born harmonious Sisters, Voice, and Verse,
> Wed your divine sounds, and mixed power employ
> Dead things with inbreathed sense able to pierce,
> And to our high-raised phantasie present,
> That undisturbed Song of pure concent,
> Ay sung before the saphire-colored throne
> To him that sits thereon
> With Saintly shout, and solemn Jubily,
> Where the bright Seraphim in burning row
> Their loud up-lifted Angel trumpets blow,
> And the Cherubick host in thousand choirs
> Touch their immortal Harps of golden wires,
> With those just Spirits that wear victorious Palms,
> Hymns devout and holy Psalms
> Singing everlastingly;

> That we on Earth with undiscording voice
> May rightly answer that melodious noise;
> As once we did, till disproportioned sin
> Jarred against natures chime, and with harsh din
> Broke the fair musick that all creatures made
> To their great Lord, whose love their motion swayed
> In perfect Diapason, whilst they stood
> In first obedience, and their state of good.
> O may we soon again renew that Song,
> And keep in tune with Heaven, till God ere long
> To his celestial consort us unite,
> To live with him, and sing in endless morn of light.[21]

[21] "At a solemn Musick," in Ibid., I, 27ff.

There are two interesting passages which are concerned with the actual music of the service, first from the poem, "Il Penseroso":

> But let my due feet never fail,
> To walk the studious Cloisters pale,
> And love the high embowed Roof,
> With antique Pillars massy proof,
> And storied Windows richly dight,
> Casting a dim religious light.
> There let the pealing Organ blow,
> To the full voiced Choir below,
> In Service high, and Anthems clear,
> As may with sweetness, through mine ear,
> Dissolve me into extasies,
> And bring all Heaven before mine eyes.[22]

[22] "Il Penseroso," in Ibid., I, 45.

In his "Eikonoklastes," Milton reflects on the joy and gladness "between the Singing men and the organs" of the king's chapel. He cannot help but wonder, however, in a reference to Latin texts, "how they should join their hearts in unity to songs not understood."[23]

[23] "Eikonoklastes," in Ibid., V, 263.

Another religious theme, under which Milton discusses music at length, is the creation of the world. In his "Paradise Lost," on the seventh day God rested, but, says Milton, he did not rest in silence.

> But not in silence holy kept; the Harp
> Had work and rested not, the solemn Pipe,
> And Dulcimer, all Organs of sweet stop,

> All sounds on Fret by String or Golden Wire
> Tempered soft Tunings, intermixt with Voice
> Choral or Unison ...
> Creation and the six Days acts they sung ...[24]

[24] Ibid., VII, 594ff.

After God tells Adam he must leave Eden, the angel, Michael, leads Adam to the top of a high hill where he can see visions of the future. Among the things predicted for the future, Adam hears music.

> Whence the sound
> Of Instruments that made melodious chime
> Was heard, of Harp and Organ; and who moved
> Their stops and chords was seen: his volant touch
> Instinct through all proportions low and high
> Fled and pursued transverse the resonant fugue.[25]

[25] "Paradise Lost," XI, 558ff, in Ibid., II, 365.

Adam, in these same visions, also hears the "Carol" which the angels sang, announcing the birth of Jesus.[26]

[26] Ibid., XII, 365.

In the continuation of his story of man, in "Paradise Regained," God announces he will create a son "of female Seed" to "earn Salvation for the Sons of men." Upon this announcement, celestial music is heard.

> So spake the Eternal Father, and all Heaven
> Admiring stood a space, then into Hymns
> Burst forth, and in Celestial measures moved,
> Circling the Throne and Singing, while the hand
> Sung with the voice, and this the argument.
> Victory and Triumph to the Son of God
> Now entering his great duel, not of arms,
> But to vanquish by wisdom hellish wiles.[27]

[27] "Paradise Regained," I, 168ff, in Ibid., II, 411.

Later Satan takes Jesus up on a mountain to show him the kingdoms he may posses if he follows Satan. Among the visions shown Jesus we find,

> And all the while Harmonious Airs were heard
> Of chiming strings, or charming pipes and winds.[28]

[28] Ibid., II, 362.

In reference to the schools of ancient Greece, Satan promises Jesus he shall learn the secret power of music.

> There thou shalt hear and learn the secret power
> Of harmony in tones and numbers hit
> By voice or hand, and various-measured verse,
> *Aeolian* charms and *Dorian* Lyric Odes ... [29]

Milton delighted in describing the music of angels. In a poem, "Upon the Circumcision," Milton portrays the singing of the angels who announced the birth of Jesus.

> Ye flaming Powers, and winged Warriours bright,
> That erst with Musick, and triumphant song
> First heard by happy watchful Shepherds ear,
> So sweetly sung your Joy the Clouds along
> Through the soft silence of the listening night.[30]

His "Paradise Lost," has several descriptions of the heavenly music of angels, for example:

> Then Crowned again their golden Harps they took,
> Harps ever tuned, that glittering by their side
> Like Quivers hung, and with Preamble sweet
> Of charming symphonie they introduce
> Their sacred Song, and waken raptures high;
> No voice exempt, no vice but well could join
> Melodious part, such concord is in Heaven.[31]

Angels, whom Milton describes as "millions of spiritual Creatures" who "walk the Earth Unseen, both when we wake, and when we sleep," perform both vocal and instrumental music.

> Celestial voices to the midnight air,
> Sole, or responsive each to others note
> Singing their great Creator: oft in bands
> While they keep watch, or nightly rounding walk
> With Heavenly touch of instrumental sounds
> In full harmonic number joined, their songs
> Divide the night, and lift our thoughts to Heaven.[32]

One of the fallen angels in "Paradise Lost" contemplates being reinstated and having to celebrate God "with warbled hymns, and to his Godhead sing forced Hallelujahs."[33]

> Speak ye who best can tell, ye Sons of light,

---

[29] Ibid., IV, 254.

[30] "Upon the Circumcision," in Ibid., I, 26.

[31] "Paradise Lost," in III, 365ff, Ibid., II, 90.

[32] "Paradise Lost," in IV, 682ff, Ibid., II, 130ff. Celestial Choirs are mentioned again in Book VII, 254.

[33] "Paradise Lost," II, 240ff, in Ibid., II, 46.

Angels, for ye behold him, and with songs
And choral symphonies, Day without Night,
Circle his Throne rejoicing ... [34]

[34] "Paradise Lost," V, 160ff, in Ibid., II, 149.

Finally, there are some interesting and humorous references to the general deportment in the church service, which, if these views were commonly held, might have added support to the complaints of the Puritans. First, Thomas Dekker (1570–1630) describes the manners of the courtier in church.

> Never be seen to mount the steps into the choir, but upon
> a high Festival day, to prefer the fashion of your doublet,
> and especially if the singing-boys seem to take note of you:
> for they are able to buzz your praises above their Anthems,
> if their voices have not lost their maidenheads: but be sure
> your silver spurs dog your heels, and then the Boyes will
> swarm about you like so many white butter-flyes, when you
> in the open Choir shall draw forth a perfumed embroidered
> purse (the glorious sight of which will entice many Country-
> men from their devotion to wondering) and quoyt silver
> into the Boyes hands, that it may be heard above the first
> lessons, although it be read in a voice as big as one of the
> great Organs.
>
> This noble and notable Act being performed, you are to
> vanish presently out of the Choir, and to appear again in the
> walk.[35]

[35] Thomas Dekker, "The Guls Horn-Booke" (1609).

4
Music in Jacobean Society

> Lord, place me in Thy concert; give one strain
> To my poor reed!
> *George Herbert (1593–1633)*[1]

THE PURPOSE HERE is to seek clues in fictional literature which might offer insight to the general familiarity with music by English society at large. We begin with observations by playwrights who are concerned with the decline of music and the arts. We see this in Jonson's tragedy, *Sejanus* (I, i), where Sabinus observes,

> We [lack] the fine arts and their thriving use,
> Should make us graced, or favored of the times,

and with regard to music in particular in the "To the Readers of this Comedy" in Beaumont and Fletcher's *The Knight of the Burning Pestle*.

> Gentlemen, the World is so nice in these our times, that for Apparel, there is no fashion, For Musick, which is a rare Art, (though now slighted) No Instrument ...

During much of the fifteenth and sixteenth centuries the ability to sing and perform on a musical instrument was considered a necessary accomplishment of a gentleman. In England at the end of the sixteenth century this begins to change, although we find a few references in the early

---

[1] "Employment," in *The Poems of George Herbert*, ed. Ernest Rhys (London: Walter Scott, 1885), 51. George Herbert devoted most of his poetry to the Church of England, which he served as a rector near Salisbury. None of his poetry was published during his lifetime. Some publications refer to him as a "late orator of the University of Cambridge."

seventeenth century plays which still refer to the gentleman as an amateur musician. In Beaumont and Fletcher's *The Loyal Subject* (II, i) a character called Ancient, who identifies himself as a soldier and a gentleman, sings a song and then observes,

> 'Tis a singing age Sir,
> A merry moon here now: I'le follow it:
> Fidling, and fooling now, gains more than fighting.

In another play by these authors, *The Coronation* (I, i), the Queen agrees that the qualities of the Gentleman include dancing, singing and playing the lute. On the other hand, these qualities may not be appropriate for a guard, for

> How can he stand
> Upon his guard, who hath Fidlers in his head,
> To which, his feet must ever be a dancing?

Passarello, an entertainer attached to Bilioso, an old marshal, in Marston's *The Malcontent* (I, iii), suggests the gentleman did not sing well.

> Yes, I can sing, fool, if you'll bear the burden; and I can play upon instruments, scurvily, as gentlemen do.

Roger North (1653–1734), an amateur musician born to a well-to-do family and educated in law, brought to his writing a breadth of knowledge not enjoyed by his contemporaries who wrote on music and who were primarily working musicians. English literature of the late sixteenth century had been strongly critical of young men who, upon completion of the university, went to Italy to "complete" their education as a gentleman. It is interesting therefore, that North not only approved such travel to Italy, once referring to her as "Italy, where music is queen,"[2] but attributed to this exposure an important influence on English music.

[2] Quoted in John Wilson, *Roger North on Music* (London: Novello, 1959), 9.

> The other circumstance I hinted was the numerous train of young travelers of the best quality & estates, that about this time went over into Italy & resided at Rome & Venice, where they heard the best music and learned from the best

masters ... and they came home confirmed in the love of the Italian manner, & some contracted no little skill & proved exquisite performers; then came over Corelli's first consort that cleared the ground of all other sorts of music whatsoever; by degrees the rest of his consorts & at last the concerti came, all of which are to the musicians like the bread of life.[3]

[3] Roger North, *The Musicall Gramarian* (Oxford: Oxford University Press, 1925), 37.

In another place, however, North seems to have come to doubt the long-range value of this study in Italy. In the following, he appears to suggest that he regrets the old common style passed by in favor of music being developed as an aesthetic art. He would not have disagreed if one phrased it instead, the good old English music is being displaced by Italian taste.

> As Rome was destroyed by the Asiatic luxury, so the musical republic will sink to nothing under the weight of these numerous curiosities lately brought over it. The flourishing of an art or science, is the number and value of the professors, and those obtaining their end, which in music is pleasure, and an innocuous employ of spare time, with a recreation, in the intervals of business, the gain and credit is egregious; all which fell out when the art was plain and practicable and most sober families in England affected it. Now it is come to that pass, that few but professors can handle it, and the value is derived upon high flights & numbers of capital performers, which may have brought an audience but the promiscuous and diffused practice of music in remote parts about England is utterly confounded. And an ostentatious pride hath taken Apollos' chair and almost subverted his monarchy.[4]

[4] Ibid., 41.

One clear indication of the familiarity of music by at least the educated class can be found in the frequent instances of humor, metaphors and other figures of speech which required some knowledge of music to be understood. The significance of this is perhaps best seen in the fact that virtually nothing of this nature is routinely found in the theater today.

Regarding the use of music in a humorous context, we mention only two examples. First, humor based on the confusion of the senses is found in Marston's play, *Antonio and Mellida*, Part II (III, ii), when Balurdo enters with a bass viol and says, "I have the most respective fiddle; did you ever smell a more sweet sound?" The second example involves a play on the word "noise," which the early seventeenth century audience understood to be a synonym for instrumental music. In Jonson's comedy, *The Silent Woman*, Act III, scene vii begins,

> CLERIMONT. By your leave, ladies. Do you want any music? I have brought you variety of noises. Play, sirs, all of you.
>
> *[Music of all sorts]*
>
> MOROSE. Oh, a plot, a plot, a plot, a plot upon me! This day I shall be their anvil to work on, they will grate me asunder 'Tis worse than the noise of a saw.
> CLERIMONT. No, they are hair, rosin, and guts. I can give you the receipt.
> TRUEWIT. Peace, boys.
> CLERIMONT. Play, I say.

Nothing makes the point more than the use of music as a metaphor, for without an understanding of music the entire meaning is lost. Among the numerous examples of the use of music as a metaphor, found in the Jacobean plays, we might begin with the famous metaphor coined by Plato, by which "harmony" was used to represent the healthy, well-adjusted body. Two examples in this literature which are used in the Platonic sense are found in Middleton's *Michaelmas Term* (I, i),

> STALEWOOD. Faith, like a lute that has all the strings broke; nobody will meddle with her.
> REARAGE. Fie, there are doctors now in town will string her again, and make her sound as sweet as ever she did.[5]

and in Chapman's *The Blind Beggar* (Scene iii), when Leon observes,

> Love decks the countenance, spiriteth the eye,
> And tunes the soul in sweetest harmony.

George Wither, in one of his poems, uses this same metaphor to reflect the health of the state, rather than of the person.

---

[5] Perhaps another example of this kind is found in Thomas Middleton's *The Phoenix*, which ends with, "In my blood peace's music..."

Musique may teach of difference in degree,
The best tuned Common-Weales will framed be.[6]

[6] *Wither*, Spenser Society, Nr. 10, "Epithalamia," 465.

A similar sentiment is made by John Suckling, in his New Year's poem to the king in 1640:

May all the discords in your state
(Like those in music we create)
Be governed at so wise a rate,
That what would of itself sound harsh, or fright,
May be so tempered that it may delight.[7]

[7] *The Works of Sir John Suckling*, ed. Hamilton Thompson (New York: Russell & Russell, 1964), 15. Sir John Suckling (1609–1642), associated with the "Cavalier Poets," was a notorious gambler and courtier of Charles. He was forced to flee to France where he took his own life.

An example of a metaphor in which music represents "out of tune" health can be found in the play, *Every Man out of his Humour* (III, ix). Here, Jonson presents a scene in a room at court and Fastidius sings to Saviolina, accompanying himself on a viol.

FASTIDIUS. By the soul of music, lady (*hum, hum*).
SAVIOLINA. Would we might hear it once.
FASTIDIUS. I do more adore and admire your (*hum, hum*) predominant perfections than (*hum, hum*) ever I shall have power and faculty to express (*hum*).
SAVIOLINA. Upon the viol de gambo, you mean?
FASTIDIUS. It's miserably out of tune, by this hand.
SAVIOLINA. Nay, rather by the fingers.
MACILENTE. [*Aside*] It makes good harmony with her wit.

A frequent figure of speech is the use of music as a metaphor for the state of being pleased. This is the meaning of an expression in Dekker's *The Roaring Girl* (V, ii) when Alexander says, "I finde it in the musicke of my heart." In Cyril Tourneur's, *The Atheist's Tragedy*, we find an unusual example of this kind of metaphor[8] in Act V, which begins with the stage direction "music." D'Amville doesn't appreciate the music, saying "Cease that harsh music," but when he picks up some gold, he uses music as a metaphor for his pleasure.

[8] Cyril Tourneur surfaces as a writer in 1613, before which little is known. He accompanied Sir Edward Cecil on several sea voyages and died in Ireland in 1626 of an unknown disease acquired at sea.

Here sounds a music whose melodious touch
Like angels' voices ravishes the sense.

In Dekker's *The Honest Whore*, Part II (V, ii), we find the earliest version that we know of a now familiar figure of speech. Bellafront says,

> Let mercy touch your heart-strings gracious Lord
> That it may sound like musike in the eare
> Of a man desperate ...

Aside from its metaphorical usage, it is an odd expression. Is the alternative "music for the eye?" We wonder if in some way this expression had its roots in the Scholastic university distinction of "speculative" and "practical" music, which, as in universities today, meant one kind of music for the eye and another for the ear. We should also point out that Dekker corrects this medieval misunderstanding in his *The Witch of Edmonton* (III, iii), when Old Carter makes the observation, "There's no musick but in sound, sound it must be."

Music is also used as a metaphor for various aspects of speech. Two usages which are familiar today are found in Heywood's *The Golden Age*,[9] when Jupiter observes "Womens tongues and hearts have different tunes," and in Chapman's *All Fools* (V, ii), where "sing your old song no more," is used for an often repeated phrase. In Chapman's *Bussy D'Ambois* (I, ii), there is a similar metaphor for one who speaks well. Bussy says to Pyra, a court lady, "your descants do marvelous well fit this ground." We might also mention two lines which appear later (IV, i), when Tamyra observes,

> You could all this time be at concord with him,
> That still hath played such discords on your honor.

We also find music used as a metaphor for various aspects of time. In Beaumont and Fletcher's *The Little Thief* (Act III), music is used as a metaphor for "time to get organized."

> And tune our Instruments till the Consort come
> To make up the full noise ...

In Middleton's *A Fair Quarrel* (I, i) we find music used as a metaphor by Russell to express to two gentlemen that it is the wrong time to duel. Put your swords away, he says,

> Hide 'em, for shame! I had thought soldiers
> Had been musical, would not strike out of time,
> But to the consort of drum, trumps, and fife:

---

[9] *The Dramatic Works of Thomas Heywood* (New York: Russell & Russell, 1964), III, 68. This edition is a reprint of an 1874 one which, in a misguided attempt to ease the reading, omitted all references to scenes and most Acts. Therefore we cite page numbers.

'Tis madmen-like to dance without music,
And most unpleasing shows to the beholders,
A Lydian verse to a Doric note.

For a final example from the plays, we mention a line which would have been humorous to a university student of music. In a humorous scene in Middleton's *Your Five Gallants* (II, i) a "music house" is used as a metaphor for a house of prostitution. Among the dialog of three young "gallants," we find,

> PRIMERO. La, I tell you;—you'll bear me witness, gentlemen,
>   If their complaints come to their parents' ears,
>   They're words of art I teach 'em, nought but art.
> GOLDSTONE. Why, 'tis most certain.
> BUNGLER. For all [students] know that *musica est ars.*

There are some additional interesting examples of music used as a metaphor to be found in the poetry of the seventeenth century in England. Thomas Carew uses the metaphor of harmony to represent the sum of the features of the face of a lady recently deceased.

> The harmony of colors, features, grace,
> Resulting Aires (the magicke of a face)
> Of musical sweet tunes, all which combined
> To this dark Vault.[10]

The trumpet as a metaphor for an important communication was used a number of times by these poets. Perhaps there are no better representatives than those found in the poetry of King James I himself. One reads,

> So Homer was a sounding trumpet fine
> Amongst the Greeks into his learned days ...[11]

The king used this same metaphor in another work, the fragment of a wedding poem.

> Which by the trumpet of my verse I made for to resound
> From pole to pole through every where of this immobile
>   round.[12]

---

[10] Thomas Carew, "Epitaph on the Lady S.," in *The Poems of Thomas Carew*, ed. Rhodes Dunlap (Oxford: Clarendon Press, 1964), 55. Thomas Carew (1594–1639), one of the "Cavalier" poets, was trained in law but gained his reputation as a poet among the upper class.

[11] "A Sonnet," in *New Poems of James I*, ed. Allan Westcott (New York: AMS Press, 1966), 29.

[12] "An Epithalamion," in Ibid., 47.

Of course, the most familiar figure of speech involving the trumpet is its use as a metaphor for the Day of Judgment. In Richard Crashaw we also get some description of its sound on that august day.

> O that trump! whose blast shall run
> An even round with the circling Sun.[13]

[13] "In Meditation of the Day of Judgment," in *The Complete Poetry of Richard Crashaw*, ed. George Williams (New York: New York University Press, 1972), 189. A similar use of this metaphor is found in "An Elegie on my Muse," in *The Complete Poetry of Ben Jonson*, ed. William Hunter (New York: Norton, 1963), 258.

In Jonson's plays we find two references of the gentleman which are related to university life. In the literature of the late sixteenth century in England there was much criticism of the universities for allowing young men to indulge in poetry, rather than in more important subjects. It is in this perspective that we find in *Every Man in his Humour* (I, i), an old gentleman, Knowell (a pun, of course), who observes,

> Myself was once a student; and, indeed,
> Fed with the selfsame humour he is now,
> Dreaming on naught but idle poetry,
> That fruitless and unprofitable art,
> Good unto none, but least to the professors,
> Which then, I thought the mistress of all knowledge:
> But since, time, and the truth have waked my judgment,
> And reason taught me better to distinguish
> The vain from the useful learnings.

In his *The Staple of News* (I, v), Jonson is more indulgent when a young man is described,

> A pretty scholar, and a Master of Arts,
> Was made or went out Master of Arts in a throng,
> At the university; as before, one Christmas,
> He got into a masque at court, by his wit,
> And the good means of his cithern, holding up thus
> For one o'the music. He's a nimble fellow!

The plays also give witness to the fact that music was included in the skills of the well-educated young lady at this time. Middleton refers to this in three separate plays,[14] first in *Women Beware Women* (III, ii), where Fabricio observes,

[14] Thomas Middleton's *A Chaste Maid in Cheapside* begins with Maudlin asking her daughter, Moll, if she has played her virginal lessons and practiced her dancing.

> She has the full qualities of a gentlewoman;
> I've brought her up to music, dancing, what not,
> That may commend her sex, and stir her husband.

In *No Wit, no Help Like a Woman's* (IV, i), Sir Twilight commends his daughter as a "proper gentlewoman" who,

> Sings, dances, plays,
> Touches an instrument with a motherly grace.

And in *A Trick to Catch the Old One* (I, ii) a young lady is described as having been sent to London,

> to learn fashions, practice music; the voice between her lips, and the viol between her legs, she'll be fit for a consort very speedily.

In Heywood's *A Woman Kilde with Kindnesse*,[15] Charles says of a bride to be,

[15] *The Drammatic Works of Thomas Heywood*, II, 93.

> First her Birth
> Is Noble, and her education such
> As might become the Daughter of a Prince,
> Her owne tongue speakes all tongues, and her owne hand
> Can teach all strings to speake in their best grace
> From the shrill treble, to the hoarsest base.

In Beaumont and Fletcher's *The Womans Prize* (III, i), we find music used as a metaphor for four important characteristics of a young woman.

> TRANIO. Tell me but this; what dost thou think of women?
> ROWLAND. Why, as I think of Fiddles, they delight me,
>   Till their strings break.
> TRANIO. What strings?
> ROWLAND. Their Modesties,
>   Faiths, Vows, and Maidenheads, for they are like Kits
>   That have but four strings to 'em.

In another play, *The Loyal Subject* (III, vi), these authors address this topic in a humorous vein. Alinda, son of a Russian general, is coaching a young lady, Honora, on the skills she will need.

> ALINDA. Play with your Bracelets, sing: you must learn to rhyme too,
>   And riddle neatly; studie the hardest language,
>   And 'tis no matter whether it be sense, or no,
>   So it go seemlie off ...
> HONORA. Have ye schools for all these mysteries?
> ALINCA. O yes.

A poem by Ben Johnson celebrating New Year's Day, if we read it correctly, seems to be saying to the young lady, again using music as a metaphor, that what she presently knows is "today," but she must continue her education to be prepared for "tomorrow."

> New yeares, expect *new* gifts: Sister, your harp,
> Lute, lyre, theorbo, all are called today.
> Your change of Notes, the *flat*, the *meane*, the *sharpe*,
> To show the rites, and to usher forth the way.[16]

[16] *The Complete Poetry of Ben Jonson*, 241.

A poem by George Withers, a strong Puritan, finds fault with the musicians, many of whom were classified as courtiers, for moving so easily from "today" to "tomorrow," politically. He complains that the musicians who so eagerly wrote "their lyrics, heroic poems and odes" for Cromwell, now after his fall immediately changed their colors and returned to composing for the new king.

> Yea, all her Songs unto this present day,
> Are but the same, new set another way:
> And, their composers do deserve no more
> Than *begging Fiddlers* begging at the door.
> Who if it might their servile ends advance,
> Would, to the same tune play the devil a dance.[17]

[17] *Works of George Wither* (New York: Franklin, 1967), Nr. 22, "Speculum Speculativum," 71. George Wither (1588–1667), one of the so-called Cavalier Poets, was an officer in the Puritan army and most of his poetry is political in nature.

As in the sixteenth century, the Jacobean playwrights somewhat ridicule that special class of gentleman known as the courtier. This being the case, references to music and the arts are also often presented in humorous contexts when associated with the court and the courtier.

In Dekker's *The Wonder of a Kingdom* (III, i) a courtier places "the rarest musicians" in a category with cooks and the "fairest girles, that will sell sinne for gold." In another play by Dekker, *The Roaring Girl* (IV, i), we find,

ALEXANDER. What is he there?
SEBASTIAN. A Gentleman, a musitian sir, one of excellent fingering.
ALEXANDER. *[Aside]* Aye, I think so, I wonder how they scapt her.
SEBASTIAN. Has the most delicate stroke sir.

ALEXANDER. *[Aside]* A stroke indeed, I feel it at my heart.
SEBASTIAN. Puts down all your famous musitians.
ALEXANDER. *[Aside]* Aye, a whore may put down a hundred of them.

We have mentioned above, the Scholastic division of music into the "speculative" and the "practical." Jonson satirizes this idea in a pedagogy for the courtier's practice of facial expressions in his comedy, *Cynthia's Revels* (II, iii).

> But now, to come to your face of faces, or courtier's face, 'tis of three sorts, according to our subdivision of a courtier, elementary, practic, and theoric. Your courtier theoric is he that hath arrived to his farthest, and doth now know the court rather by speculation than practice; and this is his face: a fastidious and oblique face, that looks as it went with a vice, and were screwed thus. Your courtier practic is he that is yet in his path, his course, his way, and hath not touched the punctilio, or point of his hopes; his face is here: a most promising, open, smooth, and overflowing face, that seems as it would run and pour itself into you. Somewhat a northerly face. Your courtier elementary is one but newly entered, or as it were in the alphabet, or *ut-re-mi-fa-sol-la* of courtship. Note well this face, for it is this you must practice.[18]

We are fond of a passage in Beaumont and Fletcher's *The Elder Brother* (I, ii), where a young lady, Angellina, is explaining her rather modern requirements in a husband:

> ANGELLINA. Troth as of the Courtier, all his Songs and Sonnets, his Anagrams, Acrosticks, Epigrams, his deep and Philosophical Discourse of Nature's hidden Secrets, makes not up a perfect Husband ... No, no, Father, though I could be well pleased to have my Husband a Courtier, and a Scholar, young, and valiant; these are but gawdy nothings, if there be not something to make a substance.
> LEWIS. And what is that?
> ANGELLINA. A full Estate, and that said, I've said all; and get me such a one with these Additions, farewell Virginity ...

In Chapman's *Bussy D'Ambois* (I, ii), we find a specific reference to the courtier's ability to play a string instrument.

> TAMYRA. The man's a courtier at first sight.
> BUSSY. I can sing prick-song, lady, at first sight; and why not be a courtier as suddenly?

[18] In Jonson's comedy *The Silent Woman* (V, ii) Centaur observes of a court lady, "she is a perfect courtier, and loves nobody, but for her uses: and for her uses, she loves all."

In Chapman's *All Fools* (II, i), there is a very interesting, and unusually lengthy, discussion of the cultural training of the young courtier, in this case Valerio, son to a knight. Cornelio, a gentleman aspiring to be more active in the court, begins by commenting on how much he admires Valerio for his self-education, which includes music.

> He has stolen languages, Italian, Spanish
> And some spice of the French, besides his dancing,
> Singing, playing on choice instruments ...

Valerio modestly responds,

> Toys, toys, a pox; and yet they be such toys,
> As every Gentleman would not be without.

He is asked to demonstrate his musical skills, but pleads he is out of shape.

> CORNELIO. Prythee Val,
>   Take thy Theorbo for my sake a little.
> VALERIO. By heaven, this month I touched not a Theorbo.
> CORNELIO. Touched a Theorbo? marke the very word.
>   Sirra, go fetch.

> *Exit Page.*

> VALERIO. If you will have it, I must needs confess,
>   I am no husband of my qualities.

While the page goes to get a Theorbo, Valerio dances and is complimented, but he is still requested to play.

> CORNELIO. Come sweet Val, touch and sing.
> DARIOTTO. Foote, will you hear
>   The worst voice in Italy?
> CORNELIO. O God, sir.

> *[Valerio] sings.*

>   Courtiers, how like you this?
> DARIOTTO. Believe it excellent.
> CORNELIO. Is it not natural?
> VALERIO. If my father heard me,

> Foot, he'd renounce me for his natural son.
> DARIOTTO. By heaven, Valerio, and I were thy father,
> And loved good qualities as I do my life,
> I'd disinherit thee: for I never heard
> Dog howl with worse grace.
> CORNELIO. Go to, Courtier,
> You deal not courtly now to be so plain,
> Nor nobly, to discourage a young Gentleman,
> In virtuous qualities, that has but stolen them.

Later (III, i) the Page offers the courtiers advice on the proper treatment of women, which is basically to keep them in the home, busy with "sowing, singing, playing [instruments], childing, dancing, or so on."

5
Music in the Jacobean Theater

JACOBEAN THEATER is represented by the generation of playwrights after the great period of Elizabethan theater at the end of the sixteenth century. If this repertoire contains no playwright of the stature of Marlowe or Shakespeare, nevertheless this literature offers many insights into music values at the beginning of the seventeenth century in England. While the artistic value of this literature does not equal that of the Elizabethan, it was more popular. The Globe Theater, after it was rebuilt in 1613, held two thousand spectators and by 1631 there were seventeen theaters in or near London. The increased number of spectators was due in large part to the fact that the plays were mostly now comedies, as is mentioned in the Prologue of Thomas Dekker's *The Roaring Girle*.

> Shall fill with laughter our vast Theater,
> That's all which I dare promise: Tragick passion,
> And such grave stuffe, is this day out of fashion.[1]

On the Purpose of Music

IN TOURNEUR'S *The Atheist's Tragedy* (III, iii), we find the observation that music *must* have a purpose. Sebastian, in the course of using music as metaphor for Charlemont's

---

[1] Thomas Dekker (b. 1570) was a very fluent writer, producing plays of his own and in collaboration with others, in addition to "entertainments" and pamphlets on a variety of subjects. It has been said that no writer gave a more vivid picture of London at this time. He, however, failed to earn a living and was often in prison—once for three years. Nothing is known of him after the 1630s.

emotional state, says, "But trebles and basses make poor music without means."

The most frequently mentioned purpose of music in all early literature is to soothe the feelings of the listener, and we continue to find many such references in the Jacobean plays. In Marston's *Antonio and Mellida* (III, ii), Andrugio, Duke of Genoa, says, "My soul grows heavy: boy, let's have a song." After the stage direction, "a song," Andrugio responds,

> 'Tis a good boy, and by my troth, well sung.
> O, and thou felt'st my grief, I warrant thee ...

In another Marston play, *What You Will* (II, i), Quadratus sings of music being one of the things which ward off sorrow:

> Music, tobacco, sack, and sleep,
> The tide of sorrow backward keep.

In Beaumont and Fletcher's *The Lovers Progress* (III, i) A Friar offers to have one of his novices sing to solace Clarange, who responds,

> And it will come timely,
> For I am full of melancholy thoughts,
> Against which I have heard with reason Musick
> To be the speediest cure, pray you apply it.

The novice's song begins,

> A Dieu fond love, farewel you wanton powers,
> I am free again ...

Following the song,

> FRIAR. How do ye approve it?
> CLARANGE. It is a Heavenly Hymn, no ditty Father,
>   It passes through my ears unto my soul,
>   And works divinely on it.

In Beaumont and Fletcher's *The Spanish Curate* (III, ii), we find,

> We have brought Musick to appease his spirit,
> And the best Song we'll give him.[2]

[2] In Beaumont and Fletcher's *The Loyal Subject* (I, ii), Alinda observes she has too much grief to sing.

And in these author's *Thierry and Theodoret* (III, i), after the stage direction calls for "Soft Musick," Thierry observes, "Musick drowns all sadness."

In Heywood's *A Woman Kilde with Kindnesse*,[3] a character is impatient and threatens,

> ... quickly, if the Musicke overcome not my melancholly, I shall quarrell.

There are also, in these plays, a few instances where music fails in its purpose to soothe. In Middleton's *A Chaste Maid in Cheapside* (V, ii), a mother asks her daughter to sing a song to relieve her sorrow, but the daughter sings such a tragic song that the mother can only respond, "O, I could die with music!"

Similarly, in Heywood's *The Iron Age*, Part II,[4] a stage direction reads,

> *Musicke and healthing within.*

after which, Orestes laments,

> Oh Cethus what's this musicke unto me,
> That am composed of discords? What are healths
> To him that is struck heart-sick?

While such references to music which fails to soothe may be found in earlier literature, one almost never finds a circumstances where the music goes beyond failing to actually create an adverse effect in the listener. We find such a case in Beaumont and Fletcher's *The Coronation* (III, i), when the Queen complains,

> This is not Musick
> Sprightly enough, it feeds the soul with melancholy.

Similarly, in these author's *The Queen of Corinth* (III, ii), after the stage direction, "A sad Song,"

> Weep no more, nor sigh nor groan
> Sorrow calls no time that's gone ...
> AGENOR. These heavy Ayres feed sorrow in her Lady,
>   And nourish it too strongly; like a Mother
>   That spoiles her Child with giving on't the will.

[3] *The Dramatic Works of Thomas Heywood* (New York: Russell & Russell, 1964), II, 97. This edition is a reprint of an 1874 one which, in a misguided attempt to ease the reading, omitted all references to scenes and most acts. Therefore we cite page numbers.

[4] Ibid., III, 409.

In Dekker's *Old Fortunatus* (III, i) a boy serenades Orleans with a lute, but the latter begs him to leave, saying, "This musicke makes me but more out of tune."

Another purpose of music is to delight, or for pleasure. In the "Induction" to Marston's *What You Will*, we find,

> Music and poetry were first approved
> By common sense; and that which pleased most,
> Held most allowed pass: know, rules of art
> Were shaped to pleasure, not pleasure to your rules.

In Beaumont and Fletcher's *Wit at Several Weapons* (II, i), Cunningam reflects,

> With purpose that my harmony shall reach
> And please the Ladies ear ...

In the plays of Dekker there are also several interesting references to the purpose of music being to please. In *Westward Ho* (IV, ii), we find mention of one of the characteristics which so fascinated the ancient Greek philosophers, the fact that music is the only art which cannot be seen. Here, the Earle philosophizes,

> Go, let musicke
> Charme with her excellent voice an awfull silence
> Through all this building, that her sphaery soule
> May (on the wings of Ayre) in thousand formes
> Invisibly flie, yet be enjoyed.

In Dekker's *Old Fortunatus* (II, ii), Fortunatus observes he has been ravished with divine raptures of "Dorick, Lidian and Phrigian harmonies" and in *Lust's Dominion* (I, i) the Queen Mother says,

> Chime out your softest strains of harmony,
> And on delicious Musicks silken wings
> Send ravishing delight to my loves ears,
> That he may be enamored of your tunes.

The most important and fundamental purpose of music is as a special language to express feelings. Among the passages in this literature which interest us in this regard, we first notice a reference in Dekker's *The Honest Whore*, Part I (I, ii) where the very term "musician" is synonymous with an emotional person. Here a wife describes her placid husband as one who never gets upset with servants, has no more sting than an ant, etc., thus she concludes a "Musitian will he never be." Perhaps this was also intended in Middleton's *The Witch* (II, i) when Isabella comments, "I will not grumble, sir, like some musician."

Regarding the expression of feeling through music, we especially notice some lines in Beaumont and Fletcher's *The Faithful Shepherdess* (V, i) where a Priest observes he is willing to hear a shepherd's song *only* if it is sung with feeling.

> 'Tis good to hear ye, Shepherd, if the heart
> In this well sounding Musick bear his part.

In another Beaumont and Fletcher play, *The Tragedy of Valentinian* (II, iv), just before the lyrics for songs of love, Licinius calls for music:

> She is coming up the stairs; Now the Musick;
> And as that stirs her, let's set on ...

We have an insight into the deep expressons of emotion expressed in song at this time in Marston's *Antonio and Mellida* (IV, i), in the instructions of Antonio to a Page before the latter sings.

> I prithee sing, but mark my words
> Let each note breathe the heart of passion,
> The sad extracture of extremest grief.
> Make me a strain speak groaning like a bell
> That tolls departing souls;
> Breathe me a point that may enforce me weep,
> To wring my hands, to break my cursed breast,
> Rave, and exclaim, lie grovelling on the earth,
> Straight start up frantic, crying, Mellida!
> Sing but, "Antonio hath lost Mellida,"
> And thou shalt see me like a man possess'd
> Howl out such passion, that even this brinish marsh
> Will squeeze out tears from out his spongy cheeks:
> The rocks even groan, and—prithee, prithee sing.

Another Marston play reminds us that the feelings expressed in music must be genuine. In *Antonio and Mellida*, Part II (IV, ii) Antonio, Pandulfo and Alberto enter the stage with daggers and we read,

> ANTONIO. Wilt sing a dirge, boy?
> PANDULFO. No, no song; 'twill be vile out of tune.
> ALBERTO. Indeed, he's hoarse; the poor boy's voice is cracked.
> PANDULFO. Why, coz! why should it not be hoarse and cracked,
>   When all the strings of nature's symphony
>   Are cracked and jar? Why should his voice keep tune,
>   When there's no music in the breast of man?

In Marston we also find references to the communication of feelings of love through music, as in *Antonio and Mellida* (III, ii), where Castillo makes plans, before a song.

> I will warble to the delicious conclave of my mistress' ear: and strike her thoughts with the pleasing touch of my voice.

In another play, Marston speaks of music's power to inspire physical love.[5] In Marston's *The Insatiate Countess* (III, iv) Isabella calls upon the power of music.

> Harmonious music, breathe thy silver airs
> To stir up appetite to Venus' banquet,
> That breath of pleasure that entrances souls ...

In the plays of Beaumont and Fletcher we find three references to another purpose of music, music therapy. In *The Mad Lover* (IV, i), Stremon observes,

> He shall not this day perish, if his passions
> May be fed with Musick; are they ready?

And in Beaumont and Fletcher's *The Captain* (III, iv), we read,

> JULIO. What, has she musick?
> WOMAN. Yes, for Heavens sake stay,
>   'Tis all she feeds upon.

[5] In Marston's *Antonio and Mellida*, Part II (I, ii), Nutriche has a dream in which he hears three fiddlers playing a hornpipe during his seduction of a lady.

In the most famous play by these same authors, *The Knight of the Burning Pestle* (II, i), an old merchant predicts that one who laughs and sings will be protected from a wide variety of illness.

> Let each man keep his heart at ease
> No man dies of that disease,
> He that would his body keep
> From diseases, must not weep,
> But whoever laughs and sings,
> Never his body brings
> Into Fevers, Gouts, or Rhumes,
> Or lingeringly his Lungs consumes:
> Or meets with aches in the bone,
> Or Catarrhs, or griping Stone . . .

We have a rather unusual instance in Dekker's *The Wonder of a Kingdom* (III, ii), where a nurse rejects the idea of music therapy.

> THE DUKE OF FLORENCE. Call for the Musicke.
> ANGELO. Makea no noise, but bring in de Fidlers, and play sweet—
> NURSE. Oh out upon this Doctor; hang him, does he think to cure dejected Ladies with Fidlers—

An interesting example of music being used for the purpose of social protest can be found in Beaumont and Fletcher's *The Humourous Lieutenant* (II, ii). Contemplating the results of a loss in a battle, the lieutenant fears he will be the object of songs of satire.

> Now shall we have damnable Ballads out against us,
> Most wicked madrigals: and ten to one, Colonel,
> Sung to such lowsie, lamentable tunes.

Among the more functional purposes of music, we find music used to awaken a character, as the use of a cornett to awaken the sleeping Mellida in Marston's *Antonio and Mellida*, Part II (I, ii).

> ANTONIO. Boy, wind thy cornet: force the leaden gates
>   Of lazy sleep fly open with thy breath . . .

> [*One winds a cornet within*]
>
> Hark, madam, how yon cornet jerketh up
> His strain'd shrill accents in the capering air,
> As proud to summon up my bright-cheek'd love!

In Dekker's *Old Fortunatus* (III, i) the stage direction calls for "Musicke still" and Shaddow prepares to wake Andelocia.

> Musicke? O delicate warble: O these Courtiers are most sweete triumphant creatures. Seignior, Sir: Monsieur: sweete Seignior; this is the language of the accomplishment: O delicious strings: these heavenly wire-drawers have stretched my master even out of length: yet at length he must wake: master?

Reference to music used for a coronation is found in Dekker's *Sir Thomas Wyatt* (I, i), when Northumberland says,

> Trumpets and Drums, with your notes resound,
> Her royal name, that must in state be crowned.

Later (II, ii), regarding the coronation procession, we read,

> The streets are full, the town is populous,
> The people gape for noveltie. Trumpets speak to them,
> That they may answer with an echoing crie,
> God save Queene Jane, God save her Majestie.

Finally, we read of a trumpet giving the signal for dinner in Dekker's *The Wonder of a Kingdom* (IV, ii).

On the Incidental Music in the Plays

This practice was still sufficiently common that in a rare play which did not use incidental music,[6] Heywood's *The English Traveller*, the playwright felt compelled to make an explanation in the Prologue.

> A Strange Play you are like to have, for know,
> We use no Drum, nor Trumpet, nor Dumbe show;
> No Combat, Marriage, not so much today,

[6] Thomas Heywood, in his *An Apology for Actors*, tells of an incident in 1600 when invading Spaniards, landing and hearing the trumpets and drums participating in a play given in a coastal town, believed they had been discovered and fled.

As song, Dance, Masque to bumbaste out a Play;
Yet these all good, and still in frequent use
With our best Poets; nor is this excuse
Made by our Author, as if want of skill
Caused this defect; it's rather his selfe will.

Nevertheless, in the dialog, when the situation involves a banquet, a character is quick to *refer* to music, commenting that there will be the "best consort in the Citie, for sixe parts."

The incidental music in the Jacobean plays serves many purposes. Often the music is required when time is needed for the entrance of characters. Thus when Cupid descends from the ceiling, the stage directions call for cornetts to play in Beaumont and Fletcher's *Cupid's Revenge* (Act II) and for recorders in Heywood's *Loves Mistris*.[7] Similarly, stage directions call for music in Middleton's *A Game of Chess*, while the various pieces enter the stage, while in Chapman's *The Widow's Tears* (III, ii),

> *Musique: Hymen descends; and six Sylvanes enter beneath ...*

Music is called for frequently to open a scene.[8] One of the more unusual instances is found in Marston's *The Malcontent*, which begins with a stage direction,

> *The vilest out-of-tune music being heard ...*

The following dialog includes,

PIETRO. Where breathes that music?
BILIOSO. The discord rather than the music is heard from the malcontent Malevole's chamber.

Similarly, music is called for to end a scene.[9]

SOME OF THESE STAGE DIRECTIONS are rather interesting in terms of the instruments used. In Marston's *The Tragedy of Sophonisba*, for example, Act I ends with the stage direction:

> *The cornets and organs playing loud full music*

[7] *The Dramatic Works of Thomas Heywood*, V, 129.

[8] See also Marston's *Antonio and Mellida* (I, i), "The cornets sound a battle within," and *The Tragedy of Sophonisba*, which begns, "Cornets sound a march."

[9] See also Beaumont and Fletcher's *The Prophetess*, with flourishes and Alarms to end scenes in IV, iv and v, and "Loud Music" which ends Marston's *Antonio and Mellida*, Part II (II, ii).

While one does not ordinarily think of the cornett as "loud music," we find this again in Marston's *Antonio and Mellida*, Part II (IV, ii), when Piero Sforza says,

> Come, despite of fate,
> Sound loudest music, let's pace out in state!
>
> *The cornets sound—Exeunt*

This same play ends with a stage direction which reads simply "A song." However, just before, Antonio gives us an insight into the kind of song intended by the playwright.

> Sound doleful tunes, a solemn hymn advance,
> To close the last act of my vengeance.

As with the Elizabethan plays, the stage directions very frequently call for music to introduce important personages to the stage. In both bodies of repertoire one comes to expect a trumpet fanfare to announce the entrance of a king. In one such instance, in Dekker's *Satiromastix* (II, i), the dialog which follows is unusually interesting.

> ALL. The King's at hand.
> TERRILL. Father the King's at hand.
>   Musicke talke louder, that thy silver voice,
>   May reach my Soveraignes eares.
> SIR VAUGHAN. I pray do so, Musitions bestir your fingers, that you may have us all by the eares.
> SIR QUINTILIAN. His grace comes, a Hall varlets, where by my men? blow, blow your colde Trumpets till they sweate; tickle them till the sound again.

One presumes, in the case of a king, that trumpets are intended even if the stage direction is not specific, as in Beaumont and Fletcher's *A King, and No King* (I, i), when the king enters,[10] the stage direction reads,

> *Enter Etc. Senet Flourish.*

It is an interesting exception, therefore, in James Shirley's *The Cardinal* (III, ii),[11] when a stage direction says simply "Hautbois," after which Antonio says, "This music speaks the

[10] In Act II, when the king again enters, the stage direction calls for a Flourish only. Similar uses in *The Mad Lover* (I, i); in *The Double Marriage* (III, i), "Flourish Cornets" for the entrance of Ferrand, Tyrant of Naples; in *Women Pleased* (V, i) a trumpet introduces a Knight.

[11] James Shirley (1596–1666), sometimes called "the last of the Elizabethans," was educated at the Merchant Taylors' School and at Oxford. Both he and his wife died as a result of the London fire of 1666.

king upon entrance." In Dekker's *The Welsh Embassador* (V, iii) the brother to the king is introduced by "Hoboyes."[12]

Queens are also entitled to trumpets and in Heywood's *If you know not me, you know no body*,[13] after the stage direction reads "Trumpets afar off," Sir Thomas Ramsie says,

> The Queene hath dined: the trumpets sound already,
> And give note of her coming.—Bid the Waits
> And Hoboyes to be ready at an instant.

In Chapman's *The Blind Beggar* (Scene ii), the queen Aegiale is brought onto the stage "with a sound of Horns," in a very rare reference to horns outside the domain of hunting. In Marston's *What You Will* (V, i) the advice is given,

> When you hear one wind a cornet, she is coming down Saint Mark's Street ...

A wide variety of other important persons are introduced with music in the Jacobean plays. These include a general in Beaumont and Fletcher's *The Double Marriage* (II, i), "Flourish. Trumpets, Cornets"; the captain of a ship in Heywood's *Fortune by Land and Sea*[14]; and recorders to introduce Venus in his *Loves Mistris*.[15]

OFTEN THE STAGE DIRECTIONS refer to a specific musical form. The most frequent of these is the Flourish, which we see contrasted with another form, the Senet, in Dekker's *Satiromastix* (III, ii).[16]

> *Trumpets sound a florish, and then a sennate: Enter King*

But there must have been a variety of kinds of Flourish, for at the conclusion of Marston's *The Tragedy of Sophonisba* we read of the cornetts playing "a short flourish," whereas his *The Tragedy of Sophonisba* Act III concludes with a stage direction for a "full" flourish.

> *With a full flourish of cornets, they depart.*

And presumably a Flourish of a different character was required in Webster's *Appius and Virginia*, when, after the

---

[12] See also Thomas Dekker's *The Noble Spanish Soldier* (I, i), "Enter in Magnificent state, to the sound of lowd musick, the King and Queene."; in *The Wonder of a Kingdom* (III, i); in George Chapman's *Alphonsus Emperor of Germany* (II, ii), "A train of ladies following with music," his *The Tragedy of Caesar and Pompey* (III, i), where the stage direction indicates not only that a trumpet announces the entrance of nobles, but also walks before them as they enter, and *The Blind Beggar* (Scene iv) when nobles enter there is an unusual reference to music in the stage direction, simply "with sound;" and Thomas Heywood's *King Edward the fourth, Part I*, [*The Dramatic Works of Thomas Heywood*, I, 58] "The Trumpets sound, and enters King Edward."

Somewhat more rare, there is no stage direction, but the equivalent in the dialog. See: "Sound drums, and trumpets for my Lord," in Thomas Dekker's *The Wonder of a Kingdom* (IV, i and V, ii); in Cyril Tourneur's, *The Revenger's Tragedy* (III, v), Hippolito says, "Music's at our ear; they come."

[13] *The Dramatic Works of Thomas Heywood*, I, 316.
[14] Ibid., VI, 413.
[15] Ibid., V, 96.

[16] See also many cornet flourishes in Marston's *Antonio and Mellida* and in his *The Malcontent* (IV, i), where a flourish by cornetts is associated with the announcement of the arrival of a military guard. In Act V of Jonson's comedy *Cynthia's Revels* in internal masque contains the numerous sounding of "flourish" and "charge," although no specific instruments are mentioned.

final line of dialog, the stage direction calls for a Flourish as a character is taken in a procession to her tomb.

George Chapman's *Revenge for Honor* (V, ii), ends with a stage direction with very unusual instrumentation, calling for a Flourish, one intended to be played by recorders.

Another musical form, which is also frequently found in the Elizabethan plays, is the Senet. We see this form in Marston's *Antonio and Mellida*, Part II (V, ii), where a stage direction reads,

> A song. The song ended the cornets sound a senet

In this scene a dance (the "measure," a stately dance) takes place, accompanied by the following stage direction which refers to the special alcoves for music, situated above and below the stage.

> *While the measure is dancing,* Andrugio's *ghost is placed betwixt the music-houses.*

It is generally presumed that the Senet and Flourish were both of a fanfare character, but there is never specific information to reveal the distinction. They are only distinguished in the terms themselves, as in Marston's *Antonio and Mellida* (I, i) where the stage direction calls for "the cornets to sound a senet" when three ladies enter the stage, but when the duke embraces them "the cornets sound a flourish."[17]

Another fanfare-type form which is frequently found in Elizabethan plays is the Tucket, whose origin was an ancient French military signal related to marching. In the Jacobean plays we find only a single instance when the stage direction reads "Sound a tucket," as characters appropriately process across the stage in Jonson's *The Case is Altered* (I, ix).

Yet another form which is used only once in this literature is the Rouse. In Jonson's comedy *The Silent Woman* (III, vii), Otter announces he has trumpeters and a drum offstage and calls for a "rouse for bold Britons."

A musical form which suggests trumpets or cornetts is the March, a form which appears in only one Jacobean play—apart from the "dead march," which was for drums. In this

[17] See also many cornett senets in Marston's *Antonio and Mellida* and a senet to open a scene in his *Antonio and Mellida*, Part II (II, i).

one play, Marston's *The Tragedy of Sophonisba*, however, the March is used in a variety of circumstances. Early in the play (I, ii), the stage direction calls for the cornets to play a march as preparations are made for a tournament. Later in this play (III, ii) the cornetts play a march for the entrance of Roman generals. In this same play (V, ii) there is a battle scene with numerous cornett marches, as well as "a march far off," a "flourish" and "a charge." After the battle the stage direction calls for "soft music," while Massinissa says to this music,

> ... sounds soft as Leda's breast
> Slide through all ears.

Still later in this play (V, iv) the cornetts play a march for a triumphal procession.

One finds an occasional Parley in these plays,[18] presumably performed by trumpets. In Beaumont and Fletcher's *The Double Marriage* (V, i) the stage directions call for "Sound a parley," and then after the discussion,

> *Alarum Flourish. Trumpets. Retreat.*

There are only a few clues to the actual musical styles of these fanfare-type performances. In Marston's *Antonio and Mellida* (I, i) a duke refers to a Flourish as "fresh" and "triumphal" and in Beaumont and Fletcher's *Four Moral Representations* such a performance is called "cheerful." Usually, however, for the trumpets the emphasis is on power. In fact, in two plays this power is equated to an earthquake! We find the actual word "earthquake" used with respect to the trumpet in Beaumont and Fletcher's *The False One* (III, ii) and again in Jonson's comedy, *The Silent Woman* (IV, ii) where the stage directions call for "trumpets sounding" to wake Morose. A few lines later Morose refers to their sound as follows:

> They have rent my roof, walls, and all my windows asunder with their brazen throats.

We also find two interesting descriptions of the trumpeter himself. In battle the trumpeter was always placed safely

[18] See also Beaumont and Fletcher's *The Humourous Lieutenant* (III, vi) and Thomas Heywood's *The foure Prentises of London*.

in the rear with the general as he was necessary for broadcasting the orders for the battle. This tradition is why, in Dekker's *Old Fortunatus* (I, ii), a character named Shaddow suggests that trumpeters had a way of being among the survivors.

> Nay by my troth, master, none flourish in these withering times, but Ancient bearers and trumpeters.

Another interesting description of a trumpeter is found in Dekker's *Westward Ho*, (I, ii), where we find what appears to be a description of a court trumpeter, as seen by one somewhat jealous of his lifestyle, "he wears good clothes, and is ranked in good company, but he does nothing."

> He came lately from the university, and loves City dames only for their victuals, he hath an excellent trick to keep Lobsters and Crabs sweet in summer...for which I do suspect he hath been Clarke to some Noblemans kitchen. I have heard he never loves any Wench.

Horns are usually mentioned in the context of hunting, as in Beaumont and Fletcher's *The Sea-Voyage* (II, i) where, after the stage direction "Horns within,"[19] a character refers to the music as "free hunters Musick." One may presume that the hunting horns played recognizable signals, which no doubt explains an occasional reference to cornetts playing *like* horns. In Beaumont and Fletcher's *The Two Noble Kinsmen* (III, i) after "Wind horns" several times, one finds "Wind horns of Cornets" and in Marston's *The Malcontent* (III, ii), in a scene set in a forest, a stage direction reads,

> *Cornets like horns within*

The same was undoubtedly true of trumpet signals, for in Beaumont and Fletcher's *The Prophetess* (IV, iv), the stage direction calls for "A Trumpet," Aurelia recognizes it as "A *Roman* Trumpet!"

Trombones rarely appear in the Jacobean plays by name, although there are additional occasions in which "solemn music," a common synonym for trombones, is used. The

[19] Similar instances of "wind horns" in Beaumont and Fletcher's *Thierry and Theodoret* (II, i) and *The Two Noble Kinsmen* (III, v) and in Thomas Dekker's *Patient Grissil* (I, i) and *The Shoemakers' Holiday* (II, ii); and Thomas Heywood's *A Maiden-head well lost*.

trombone consort was a standard component in official civic music of the sixteenth century and we see them in this role in Middleton's *Mayor of Queenborough* (III, iii), in a dialog between a Barber and Simon, the mayor.

> BARBER. Joy bless you, sir!
>   We'll drink your health with trumpets.
> SIMON. I with sackbuts,
>   That's the more solemn drinking for my state.

Another reference, in Beaumont and Fletcher's *The Mad Lover* (III, i), indicates drums and trombones playing together.

> *A Dead March within of Drum and Sagbutts*

After this performance, Calis asks,

> What mournfull noise is this comes creeping forward?

In both Elizabethan and Jacobean plays the oboes appear in indoor scenes, often in association with banquets as we see in Beaumont and Fletcher's *The Bloody Brother* (II, iii), where the stage direction reads,

> *Hoboys, a banquet.*

One might assume that the oboe players doubled on the flutes. In Beaumont and Fletcher's *The Maids Tragedy* (I, i), for example, we notice the stage directions call for off-stage oboes, which are soon followed by the indication of recorders.

In Dekker's *The Whore of Babylon* (Act II) there is a "dumb show," for which the stage direction reads "The Hault-boyes sound." The noble listeners are not amused.

> EMPRESS OF BABYLON. Who sets those tunes to mock us? Stay them ...
> FIRST CARDINAL. No more: your musick must be dumb.

There are numerous references to incidental music in these plays for which we read only "still music." Sometimes this seems a matter of style, as in Marston's *The Fawn* (IV, i) where the stage direction "soft music playing" is characterized in the following dialog as "music of sweetly agreeing perfection." On other occasions it seems primarily a matter of dynamics, as in Marston's *Antonio and Mellida*, Part II, (I, ii).

> PANDULFO. Entreat the music strain their instruments
> With a slight touch ...
> [*Music sounds softly*]

One case which speaks of softer dynamics is quite curious, especially as it involves a rare mention of string instruments by name.[20] In Marston's *The Tragedy of Sophonisba* (IV, i) a witch appears while a stage direction specifies,

> *Infernal music plays softly whilst Ericho enters ...*

Soon this music is heard again and now the stage direction identifies the instruments as "a treble viol, a bass lute, etc. play softly." Upon hearing this "infernal" music, Syphax observes,

> Hark! Hark! now softer melody strikes mute
> Disquiet Nature. O thou power of sound,
> How thou dost melt me! Hark! now even heaven
> Gives up his soul amongst us.

Flutes are found in association with funerals.[21] In Marston's *Antonio and Mellida* (V, i) a stage direction reads,

> *The still flutes sound a mournful senet.*
> *Enter a funeral procession.*

An interesting example, musically, is found at the conclusion of Marston's *The Tragedy of Sophonisba*, when Sophonisba's body is carried in with "mournful solemnity." For this procession the stage directions call for,

> *Organ and recorders play to a single voice.*

THE APPEARANCE OF DRUMS on both the Elizabethan and Jacobean stage was fairly common.[22] Rather unusual however is a stage direction in Beaumont and Fletcher's *The Loyal Subject* (I, iii) which calls for "Drums in cases."

---

[20] In Beaumont and Fletcher's *The Chances* (II, ii), another string instrument is mentioned, "Lute sounds within."

[21] In Marston's *Antonio and Mellida*, Part II (IV, i), before a discussion of death,"*The still flutes sound softly.*"

[22] Also see: Beaumont and Fletcher's *The Mad Lover* (I, i), [*Drums within*], and *The Pilgrim* (III, iv); Thomas Dekker: the beginning of *The Whore of Babylon* (V, iii); the end of *The Shoemakers' Holiday* (I, i); *Lust's Dominion* (IV, i and iii); *If This be not a Good Play* (IV, iii); in George Chapman's *The Blind Beggar* (Scene vii); Thomas Heywood's *The Rape of Lucrece*; *The Golden Age*; *The Iron Age*, Part II; *The foure Prentises of London*; *If you know not me, you know no body*; and a rare speaking part for a drummer in Beaumont and Fletcher's *The Two Noble Kinsmen* (III, v). The ancient pipe and tabor is mentioned in Thomas Dekker's *The Shoemakers' Holiday* (III, iii).

The one form which seems to have been associated with the drums was the "dead march."[23] A typical example is found at the beginning of Act V of Beaumont and Fletcher's *Bonduca*:

A soft dead march within.

Sometimes the stage directions call for soft drums, as in Beaumont and Fletcher's *Bonduca* (II, i), "Drum softly within," and perhaps in another work by these authors, *The Maid in the Mill* (II, v),

Drums afar off. A low March

An interesting example of soft drum playing is found in Heywood's *The foure Prentises of London*,[24] where after a stage direction reads simply "soft march," Godfrey commands,

But soft, that Drumme should speak the Pagans tongue.

The character of drum players is sometimes questioned in early literature. An example is found in Beaumont and Fletcher's *The Burning Pestle* (V, i) a cannon is not in working order and the reason given for the missing flint is "The Drummer took it out to light Tobacco."

Bagpipes appear only in Beaumont and Fletcher's *The Prophetess* (V, iii), for dancing.

There is also a single reference to a singing choir. In Beaumont and Fletcher's *Monsieur Thomas* (V, iii), after the Abbess says "to the Quire then," the stage directions read "Musick singing."

There are also instances of stage directions which call for music but do not identify the actual instruments the playwright had in mind. A typical example is Marston's *Antonio and Mellida*, Part II (I, ii), where we find,

Music sounds a short strain

Often we encounter the familiar "Loud music" or "Soft music" without further identification. In one case, in Heywood's *Loves Mistris*,[25] they seem to play at the same time. Pfiche calls "Let me hear some musicke—Loud—And Still," which is indeed followed by a stage direction reading,

[23] See also Thomas Dekker's *Sir Thomas Wyatt* (I, ii); in Cyril Tourneur's, *The Atheist's Tragedy* (III, i), for the funeral of Charlemont; Thomas Heywood's *The foure Prentises of London* [*The Dramatic Works of Thomas Heywood*, II, 178] and *If you know not me, you know no body* [Ibid., I, 238].

[24] *The Dramatic Works of Thomas Heywood*, II, 223.

[25] Ibid., V, 108.

Loude Musicke, and still Musicke.

A more philosophic example, in this regard, is found in Middleton's *The Spanish Gipsy* (III, ii). Following an off-stage flourish, Soto enters in disguise and carrying a cornett. Francisco says, "but, fellow, bring your music along with you too?" Soto responds,

> Yes, my lord, both loud music and still music; the loud is that which you have heard, and the still is that which no man can hear.

We also find some interesting examples of unidentified music which represents various aspects of the spirit world. In Beaumont and Fletcher's *The Pilgrim* (V, iv), "Musick and Birds" in the stage direction refers to music of Fairies and in Thomas Dekker's *The Virgin Martyr* (V, i) one of two references to music of the spirit world reads, "tis in the Ayre, or from some better place, a power divine."

In Heywood's *The Witches of Lancashire*[26] there is a curious and interesting scene in which the musicians who are to play for dances are apparently put under a spell and are unable to perform their duty. First, no sooner do they begin than mysteriously each player begins to play a separate, and different, tune! The stage direction reads,

> *Musicke. Every one a severall tune.*

After the guests register their dismay, the musicians are revealed in person in the "music room" above the stage. This is expressed in the program direction,

> *Musitians shew themselves above.*

The musicians now complain that though they play their string instruments, no sound comes out. The guests begin to suspect witchcraft, leading one person to observe,

> I have heard my Aunt say twenty times, that no Witchcraft can take hold of a *Lancashire* Bag-pipe, for it selfe is able to charme the Devil.

[26] Ibid., IV, 215ff.

In Dekker's *If This be not a Good Play* (I, i) begins with the stage direction,

> *Enter (at the sound of hellish musick), Pluto and Charon*

In Beaumont and Fletcher's *The Double Marriage* (II, i), strange music is heard from the sea.

> *[Strange Musick within, Hoboys.]*
> ASCANIO. Hark what noise is this?
>   What horrid noise is the Sea pleased to sing.
>   A hideous Dirge to our deliverance?
> VIROLET. Stand fast now.
>
> *[Within strange cries, horrid noise, Trumpets.]*

In another play by these authors, *The Sea-Voyage* (V, i), a phantom ship is seen, after which we find the stage direction,

> *[Horid Musick]*
> RAYMOND. What dreadful sounds are these?
> AMINTA. Infernal Musick,
>   Fit for a bloody Feast.
> ALBERT. It seems prepared
>   To kill our courages e'er they divorce
>   Our souls and bodies.

Art Music

THE STAGE PLAYS of this period are filled with songs, usually with the lyrics provided.[27]

In the plays of Marston there are frequently stage directions which simply indicate "A song within," without any clues to the character of the song. One case in which we would have liked more information regarding the nature of the music is found in *The Malcontent* (II, iii) where Mendoza stands outside the room from which the music is heard, waiting to murder Ferneze. What kind of music is heard while a character waits to kill?

To continue with this morbid line of thought, in Beaumont and Fletcher's *The Bloody Brother* (III, ii) a song is sung by a group of men about to be hanged.

[27] See also Dekker's *The Shoemakers' Holiday* (I, iv) and Heywood's *The Rape of Lucrece*, for songs sung in Dutch; Dekker's *Old Fortunatus* (I, i), for a song with chorus; Dekker's *Patient Grissil* (V, ii), for a wedding song; Dekker's *The Noble Spanish Soldier* (I, ii) a song in dialog between "Question" and "Answer"; and Middleton's *The Spanish Gipsy*, for several songs with chorus; *More Dissemblers Besides Women* (IV, i), for a Gypsy song; and *The Witch* (V, ii), for a witch's song.

> Come, Boys, sing cheerfully, we shall ne'r sing younger.
> We have chosen a loud tune too, because it should like well.

And in Webster's *The Dutchesse of Malfy* (IV, ii), a stage direction reads,

> *Here (by a Mad-man) this song is sung, to a dismall kind of Musique.*

Finally, a stage direction calls for "Soft sad music" in Ford's *The Broken Heart* (IV, iii). The lyrics for a despondent off-stage song are given, following which Orgilus observes,

> A horrid stillness
> Succeeds this deathful air . . .

As was the case with the Elizabethan theater, the subjects of the Greek myths and the ancient lyric poets are often represented in these plays. Beaumont and Fletcher's *The Faithful Shepherdess* (I, i), a pastoral play after the models of the ancient lyric poets, includes a song in praise of Pan.

> Sing his praises that doth keep
> Our flocks from harm,
> Pan the Father of our Sheep,
> And arm in arm
> Tread we softly in a round,
> Whilest the hollow neighbouring ground
> Fills the Musick with her sound.

In Heywood's *Loves Mistris*[28] there is a scene which recreates the ancient Greek myth of the musical contest between Apollo and Pan. Although in ancient literature this was an instrumental contest, here it is played out in singing, the lyrics of which are given by Heywood. At the end of this contest, Apollo passes a condemnation on Pan:

> Henceforth be all your rural musicke such,
> Made out of Tinkers, Pans, and Kettle-drummes;
> And never henceforth may your fields be graced
> With the sweet musick of Apollo's lyre.

We find a song based on the Old Testament in a text Dekker wrote for a pageant given for the inauguration of

[28] *The Dramatic Works of Thomas Heywood*, V, 123ff. Marston's *Antonio and Mellida* (V, i) has a singing contest, with the duke serving as the judge.

the Mayor of London in 1629. Included is a song about the invention of music by "Tuballcayne."[29]

[29] Genesis 4:22.

> Brave Iron! Brave Hammer! from your sound,
> The Art of Musicke has her Ground,
> On the Anvil, Thou keep'st Time …

Some songs are accompanied by the singer, as in Marston's *The Dutch Courtezan* (I, ii), when Franceschina sings an art song while accompanying herself on the lute.

There are also a number of genuine ensemble songs, an example of which is found in Jonson's comedy, *Poetaster,* at the end of Act IV, scene v. The reader will also note Crispinus's reference to vocal improvisation.

> HERMOGENES. Then, in a free and lofty strain,
>   Our broken tunes we thus repair;
> CRISPINUS. And we answer them again,
>   Running division on the panting air:
> ALBIUS. To celebrate this feast of sense,
>   As free from scandal as offense.
> HERMOGENES. Here is beauty, for the eye;
> CRISPINUS. For the ear, sweet melody;
> HERMOGENES. Ambrosiac odors, for the smell;
> CRISPINUS. Delicious nectar, for the taste;
> ALBIUS. For the touch, a lady's waist;
>   Which doth all the rest excel!

The most frequent songs, in this literature which tends toward comedy, are love songs. In Marston's *The Dutch Courtezan* (V, ii), Freevil sings a song of contemplation of love. One notices his reference to a frequent complaint among early philosophers that Reason cannot explain love.

> O Love, how strangely sweet
> Are thy weak passions!
> That love and joy should meet
> In self-same fashions!
> O who can tell
> The cause why this should move?
> But only this,—
> No reason ask of Love!

In Shirley's *The Cardinal* (V, iii) off-stage music and a love song play an unusually prominent role in establishing the background of the action to come. The characters are Placentia, a servant to a duchess, and the colonel, Hernando.

HERNANDO. What do they talk of, prithee?
PLACENTIA. His grace is very pleasant

A lute is heard.

    And kind to her; but her replies are after
    The sad condition of her sense, sometimes
    Unjointed.
HERNANDO. They have music.
PLACENTIA. A lute only.
    His grace prepared; they say, the best of Italy,
    That waits upon my lord.
HERNANDO. He thinks the duchess
    Is stung with a tarantula.
PLACENTIA. Your pardon;
    My duty is expected.

Exit.

HERNANDO. Gentle lady!—
    A voice too!

Song within.

After an off-stage song, for which the lyrics are given, Hernando continues,

    If at this distance I distinguish, 'tis not
    Church music; and the air's wanton, and no anthem
    Sung to 't, but some strange ode of love and kisses.
    What should this mean?

A few songs provide some information on aesthetic choices in song writing. First, in Jonson's comedy, *Cynthia's Revels* (IV, iii), Hedon sings a song of love:

    Oh, that joy so soon should waste!
    Or so sweet a bliss

> As a kiss
> Might not for ever last! ...
> Oh, rather than I would it smother,
> Were I to taste such another,
> It should be my wishing
> That I might die, kissing.

Hedon says he made both the verses and the music and asks Amorphus how he likes it. Amorphus answers,

> A pretty air! In general, I like it well: but in particular your long note on "die" did arride me most, but it was somewhat too long.

Amorphus offers to sing a better song, one written in honor of the lady Annabel, sister to the king of Aragon, who was thinking of him when she lay dying. According to Amorphus, as a gracious gift she left him her glove, "which golden legacy the Emperor himself took care to send after me, in six coaches, covered all in black velvet, attended by the state of his empire." In appreciation, Amorphus relates, he took up his lyra and sang this song.

> Thou more than most sweet glove
> Unto my more sweet love,
> Suffer me to store with kisses
> This empty lodging ...

When he had finished singing,

AMORPHUS. How like you it, sir?
HEDON. Very well in troth.
AMORPHUS. But very well? Oh, you are a mere mammoth rept in judgment, then. Why, do you not observe how excellently the [verse] is affected in every place? That I do not marry a word of short quantity to a long note? Nor an ascending syllable to a descending tone? Besides, upon the word "best" there, you see how I do enter with an odd minim, and drive it thorough the breve, which no intelligent musician, I know, but will affirm to be very rare, extraordinary, and pleasing.

Another reference of this sort is found in Beaumont and Fletcher's *The Elder Brother* (IV, iv).[30] Here a song is offered

[30] See also in Beaumont and Fletcher: *The Spanish Curate* (II, iv), sung with lute; *The Tragedy of Valentinian*, "Musick and Song" (V, ii), and a solo song, with chorus (V, viii); *The Chances*; *The Bloody Brother*, including a drinking song; *The Lovers Progress* (III, i), a song sung by a ghost; *The Knight of Malta* (III, i), a strophic song with four verses, sung by soldiers.

for entertainment, with the promise it will not be an "Anthem, nor one with borrowed Rhymes out of the School of Vertue." After a stage direction which reads only "A song," the listener refers to its style.

> This was never penned at Geneva, the Note's too sprightly.

Finally, in the comedy, *Poetaster*, there is a scene (II, ii) where Jonson recalls a comment frequently repeated in ancient literature, to the effect that singers never want to sing when asked, but once begun, never want to stop. Here, Hermogenes is several times begged to sing, but invariably answers only "Cannot sing." Eventually he sings and pleads to sing another song, but the company is not interested. Julia observes,

> It is the common disease of all your musicians that they know no mean, to be entreated, either to begin or end.

Later (IV, v), Hermogenes scores a nice point of his own. After making an uninvited observation, he is rebuked somewhat for speaking out of place, and answers, "Oh, 'tis our fashion to be silent when there is a better fool in place."

On Serenades

ONE CONTINUES TO FIND interesting accounts of the serenades which were mentioned so frequently in Renaissance literature.[31]

In Marston's *What You Will* (I, i) Jacomo brings his servant, Philus, to sing a serenade for him at the window of his beloved. As he hands the poem he has written to Philus to sing, Jacomo apologizes for its general lack of style, wit and for the corrections here and there.

> JACOMO. Boy, could not Orpheus make the stones to dance?
> PHILUS. Yes, sir.
> JACOMO. By our Lady, a sweet touch. Did he not bring Eurydice out of hell with his lute?
> PHILUS. So they say, sir.

[31] Additional serenades can be found in Jonson's comedy *The Devil is an Ass* (II, vi); Marston's *The Dutch Courtezan* (II, i) for a serenade with "*Pages with torches and Gentlemen with music*" and Beaumont and Fletcher's *The Little French Lawyer* (I, i), for a passing reference to a serenade as "morning musique."

JACOMO. And thou canst bring Celia's head out of the window
with thy lute. Well, hazard thy breath. Look sir, here's a
ditty.
  'Tis foully writ, slight wit, crossed here and there,
  But where thou find'st a blot, there falls a tear.

Philus sings, although Marston does not give the actual song. Jacomo complains that it is not effective because it was not sung with enough passion.

Fie! peace, peace, peace! it hath no passion in it.
O melt thy breath in fluent softer tunes,
That every note may seem to trickle down
Like sad distilling tears, and make—O God!
That I were but a poet, now to express my thoughts,
Or a musician but to sing my thoughts,
Or anything but what I am.—Sing it over once more,
My grief's a boundless sea that hath no shore.

There are two interesting descriptions of serenades in Beaumont and Fletcher. First, in *The Spanish Curate* (II, i), Leandro explains he would rather court his love by dancing and fiddling indoors, than stand in the cold and serenade her.

Or fiddle out whole frosty nights (my friends)
Under the window, while my teeth keep tune,
I hold no handsomeness. Let me get in,
There trot and fiddle where I may have fair play.

In *Wit at Several Weapons* (III, i) a page and a string player are hired to sing a serenade.

SIR GREGORY. What, are they come?
PAGE. And placed directly, Sir,
    Under the window.
SIR GREGORY. What may I call you, Gentleman?
BOY. A poor servant to the Viol, I'm the Voice, Sir.
SIR GREGORY. In good time Master Voice?
BOY. Indeed good time does get the mastery ...

The serenade itself begins,

Fain would I wake you, Sweet, but fear

I should invite you to worse cheer;
In your dreams you cannot fare
Meaner than Musick . . .

When the lady responds, the text suggests the musician was being paid by the hour.

SIR GREGORY. I hear her up, here Master Voice,
    Pay you the Instruments, save what you can . . .

On Instrumental Performances

ONE FINDS A FEW EXAMPLES of genuine instrumental performances which are descriptions of art music in this literature. In Dekker's *Satiromastix* (V, ii), after the stage direction calls for "Soft Musicke," the king reflects,

Sound Musicke, thou sweet suiter to the air,
Now woo the air again, this is the hour,
Writ in the Calender of time, this hour,
Musicke shall spend . . .

In Middleton's *A Mad World, my Masters* (II, i), we find a description of instrumental music of a "concert" nature, including a rare account in the play repertoire of a secular organ performance.

SIR BOUNTEOUS. My music! give my lord a taste of his welcome.

   *[A strain played by the consort; Sir Bounteous makes
   a courtly honor to Follywit, and seems to foot the tune.]*

   So—How like you our airs, my lord? are they choice?
FOLLYWIT. They're seldom matched, believe it . . .
SIR BOUNTEOUS. The musicians are in ordinary, yet no ordinary musicians.
   Your lordship shall hear my organs now.
FOLLYWIT. I beseech you, sir Bounteous!
SIR BOUNTEOUS. My organist!

   [The organs play]

> Come, my lord, how does your honor relish my organs?
> FOLLYWIT. A very proud air, I'faith, sir.
> SIR BOUNTEOUS. O, how can't choose? A Walloon plays upon
> 'em, and a Welchman blows wind in their breech.
>
> *[A song by the organs]*

In Beaumont and Fletcher's *The Captain* (II, ii) we find another reference to a private performance.

> FABRICIO. When is this musique?
> FREDERICK. From my Sisters chamber.
> FABRICIO. The touch is excellent, let's be attentive.
> JACOMO. Hark, are the Waits abroad?
> FABRICIO. Be softer prethee,
>   'Tis private musick.

In Marston's *The Dutch Courtezan* (III, iii) there is a possible reference to an instrumental concert, when Mulligrub says,

> Come, let's go hear some music ... Let's go hear some doleful music.

In these essays we have pointed to the presence of a contemplative listener as an essential hallmark of art music. In Marston's *Antonio and Mellida*, Part II (II, ii), a character, Piero, actually stands and listens to off-stage music:

> *A song within.—Exit Piero at the end of the song.*

In Heywood's *The Rape of Lucrece*[32] a tragic song moves one listener to tears.

[32] *The Dramatic Works of Thomas Heywood*, V, 181.

> LUCRETIUS. To these lamenting dames what canst thou sing?
>   Whose griefe through all the Romane Temples ring.

Valerius then sings a song which begins,

> Lament Ladies lament
> Lament the Roman land ...
> HORATIUS. This musicke mads me, I all mirth despise.
> LUCRETIUS. To heare him sing drawes rivers from mine eyes.

Thomas Middleton's *More Dissemblers Besides Women* begins with an off-stage song, of which Lactantio reflects,

> Welcome, soul's music! I've been listening here
> To melancholy strains from the duchess' lodgings ...

Act I, of this play, ends with another song, of which the listener, Dondolo, observes, "O rich, ravishing, rare, and enticing!" Quite different are some lines in Middleton's *Blurt, Master-Constable* (II, ii), where Imperia, a courtesan, requests happy music.

> Sing, sing, sing; some old and fantastical thing, for I cannot abide these dull and lumpish tunes; the musician stands longer a-pricking them than I would do to hear them. No, no, no, give me your light ones, that go nimbly and quick, and are full of changes, and carry sweet divisions.

We are particularly drawn to a song which concludes Jonson's comedy, *Cynthia's Revels,* and appears to refer to an Aristotelian catharsis.

> Now each one dry his weeping eyes,
> And to the well of knowledge haste;
> Where purged of your maladies,
> You may of sweeter waters taste.

6
Music in Jacobean Poetry

THE PURITAN MOVEMENT in England, which had been increasing in strength since the sixteenth century, had a significant influence on the climate for the arts. Not only did they cause the complete closing of the theaters, but music, especially that which was associated with dance, came under specific criticism. Poetry as well was attacked and even John Donne, whom many consider to be, excepting Milton, the greatest poet of the Jacobean period, seems to admit that some poetry was a "sin." He also mentions in particular, in addition to an analogy to the organ, some types of poets beneath his respect, including actors, some preachers, composers of love poetry and those who address requests to the aristocracy.

> Though Poetry indeed be such a sin
> As I think that brings dearths, and Spaniards in,
> Though like the Pestilence and old fashioned love,
> Ridingly it catch men; and doth remove
> Never, till it be [destroyed]; yet their state
> Is poor, disarmed, like Papists, not worth hate:
> One...gives idiot actors means
> (Starving himself) to live by his labored scenes.
> As in some organ, puppets dance above
> And bellows pant below, which do move.
> One would move Love by rhythms ...
> And they who write to Lords, rewards to get,
> Are they not like singers at doors for meat?[1]

[1] "Satyre II," *The Complete Poetry of John Donne* (New York: New York University Press, 1968), 18. John Donne (1573–1631) studied at both Oxford and Cambridge, but as a born Catholic was not permitted to receive a degree. After various attempts at professions brought him to poverty, he converted to the official Church, became famous for his sermons and eventually became dean of St. Paul's.

We find among these poets no specific attempt to offer a definition of music as a general topic. The nearest approach to such a topic we find in a poem by Andrew Marvell which is a virtual history of the birth of music, called "Musick's Empire."

> First was the world as one great cymbal made,
> Where jarring winds to infant Nature played;
> All musick was a solitary sound,
> To hollow rocks and murmuring fountains bound.
>
> Jubal first made the wilder notes agree,
> And Jubal tuned Musick's jubilee;
> He called the echoes from their sullen cell,
> And built the organ's city, where they dwell.
>
> Each sought a consort in that lovely place,
> And virgin trebles wed the manly bass,
> From whence the progeny of numbers new
> Into harmonious colonies withdrew;
>
> Some to the lute, some to the viol went,
> And others chose the cornet eloquent;
> These practicing the wind, and those the wire,
> To sing man's triumphs, or in heaven's choir.
>
> Then Musick, the mosaic of the air,
> Did of all these a solemn noise prepare,
> With which she gained the empire of the ear,
> Including all between the earth and sphere.[2]

The last line of the above poem was probably intended as a reference to the "Music of the Spheres," a topic which seems to have been of general interest to these poets. Some poets seem to suggest this music could actually be heard, among them Ben Jonson whose "Pastoral Dialog" begins,

> Come with our voices, let us warre,
> And challenge all the Spheres,
> Till each of us be made a Star,
> And all the world turn Ears.[3]

Robert Herrick makes a similar suggestion in his poem "To Musick. A Song."

---

[2] "Music's Empire," in *The Complete Works of Andrew Marvell* (New York: AMS Press, 1966), I, 131ff. Andrew Marvell (1621–1678) served as a secretary to Milton after the famous poet became blind.

[3] *The Complete Poetry of Ben Jonson*, ed. William Hunter (New York: Norton, 1963), 131.

> Musick, thou *Queen of Heaven*, care-charming-spel,
> That strikes a stillness in hell:
> Thou that tames Tigers, and fierce storms that rise
> With thy soul-melting Lullabies:
> Fall down, down, down, from those thy chiming spheres,
> To charm our souls, as thou enchant our ears.[4]

George Wither, on the other hand, disagrees. In his "Vaticinia Poetica," in a poem called "Song," we find,

> Sound out, ye everlasting Spheres,
> That Musick, which no mortal hears...[5]

Two poets suggest that the "Music of the Spheres" cannot be heard, but can be felt. John Donne seeks to make this point in his reference to three kinds of choirs.

> Make all this All, three Choirs, heaven, earth, and spheres,
> The first, Heaven, hath a song, but no man hears,
> The Spheres have Musick, but they have no tongue,
> Their harmony is rather danced than sung;
> But our third Choir, to which the first gives ear,
> (For, Angels learn by what the Church does here)
> This Choir hath all.[6]

Richard Crashaw, in his Hymn, "The Name of Jesus," mentions the music of the spheres, "which dull mortality more feels than hears."[7]

A common purpose of music for many persons, of course, is simply for pleasure. In this regard we notice George Wither's comments on the loss of music during the civil wars in England.

> And where sweet musique hath refresht the ear,
> Sad groans of ghosts departing, now we hear.[8]

The most frequently mentioned purpose of music in earlier literature was its capacity to soothe the feelings of the listener. Among the many poems in this literature which mention this, there is an Epigram by Ben Jonson written for the publication of a book of music by Alphonso Ferrabosco.

---

[4] Quoted in L. C. Martin, *The Poetical Works of Robert Herrick* (Oxford: Clarendon Press, 1963), 103. Herrick (1591–1674) is considered one of the most gifted of the so-called Cavalier Poets. He was a graduate of Cambridge and became a prior in Devonshire.

[5] *Works of George Wither* (New York: Franklin, 1967), Spenser Society, Nr. 26-27, Nr. 18, "Vaticinia Poetica," "Song." George Wither (1588–1667), one of the so-called Cavalier Poets was an officer in the Puritan army and most of his poetry is political in nature.

[6] "Upon the translation of the Psalmes by Sir Philip Sydney," *The Complete Poetry of John Donne*, 389. Donne also mentions the "Spheares Musick" in "Valediction of the booke," [Ibid., 117] and in his "Obsequies to the Lord Harrington" [Ibid., 260].

[7] "The Name of Jesus," in *The Complete Poetry of Richard Crashaw*, ed. George Williams (New York: New York University Press, 1972), 32. Crashaw mentions the Music of the Spheres again in his "Upon the Kings Coronation," lines 21ff; "Hymn in the Glorious Epiphanie," lines 131ff and in "The Teare" [Ibid., 51]. Henry Vaughan refers to the Music of the Spheres in his "The Tempest," in *The Works of Henry Vaughan*, ed. L. C. Martin (Oxford: At the Clarendon Press, 1957), 461. Lovelace mentions the Music of the Spheres in *The Poems of Richard Lovelace*, ed. C. H. Wilkinson (Oxford: Clarendon Press, 1930), 26, 92, 114, 160, 187.

[8] *Wither*, Spenser Society, Nr. 12, "Campo-Musae," 16.

> Which Musick had; or speake her knowne effects,
> That she removeth cares, sadness ejects,
> Declineth anger, persuades clemencie,
> Doth sweeten mirth, and heighten pietie ... [9]

[9] *The Complete Poetry of Ben Jonson*, 65.

A similar purpose is found in Thomas Carew, in a poem inspired by the illness of a friend.

> Then let the God of Musick, with still charms,
> Her restless eyes in peaceful slumbers close,
> And with soft strains sweeten her calm repose.[10]

[10] "Upon the sickness of ...," in *The Poems of Thomas Carew*, ed. Rhodes Dunlap (Oxford: Clarendon Press, 1964), 31. Thomas Carew (1594–1639), one of the "Cavalier" poets, was trained in law but gained his reputation as a poet among the upper class.

A poem by George Wither contains four lines which we really like,

> But, though that all the world's delight forsake me,
> I have a Muse, and she shall Musicke make me:
> Whose airy notes, in spite of closest cages,
> Shall give content to me, and after ages.[11]

[11] *Wither*, Spenser Society, Nr. 10, a Sonnet, in "the Shepheards Hunting," 529.

A shepherd questions if only those who sing are happy? His companion does not answer the question, but, like the old troubadours, sings of the association of music and Spring.

> WILLY. Those that sing not, must be sad?
>   Did'st thou ever that Bird hear
>   Sing well; that sings all the year?
>   Tom the Piper does not play
>   Till he wears his pipe away:
>   There's a time to slack the string,
>   And a time to leave to sing.
> PHILARETE. Yea; but no man now is still,
>   That can sing, or tune a quill.
>   Now to chant it, were but reason;
>   Song and Musicke are in season.[12]

[12] Ibid., 534ff.

At the end of the poem, Wither again returns to the ability of music to soothe.

> The Muses teach us Songs to put off cares,
> Graced with as rare and sweet conceits as theirs ... [13]

[13] Ibid., 558.

The poet, George Herbert, a rector in the Church of England, emphasized the solace to be found in church music, as he writes,

Sweetest of sweets, I thank you! when displeasure
Did through my body wound my mind,
You took me hence, and in your house of pleasure
A dainty lodging me assigned.[14]

This poet, Herbert, appears to have been a poet with considerable background in music. In his biography, by Izaak Walton, we find,

> During which time all, or the greatest diversion from his study, was the practice of music, in which he became a great master, and of which he would say, "That it did relieve his drooping spirits, compose his distracted thoughts, and raised his weary soul so far above the earth, that it gave him an earnest of the joys of heaven before he possessed them."[15]

......

> His chief recreation was music, in which heavenly art he was a most excellent master, and did himself compose many divine hymns and anthems, which he set and sung to his lute or viol; and through he was a lover of retiredness, yet his love to music was such, that he went usually twice every week on certain appointed days to the cathedral church in Salisbury; and at his return would say, that his time spent in prayer and cathedral music elevated his soul, and was his heaven upon earth. But before his return thence to Bemerton, he would usually sing and play his part at an appointed private music meeting; and, to justify this practice, he would often say, religion does not banish mirth, but only moderates and sets rules to it.

Walking once to such a chamber music rehearsal with his friends, Herbert apparently encountered a man with a horse in distress, whom he stopped to help. When his clergy friends suggested that he had "disparaged himself by so dirty an employment," he responded that,

> ... the thought of what he had done would prove music to him at midnight, and that the omission of it would have upbraided and made discord in his conscience ... "And now let us tune our instruments."

Walton tells us that days before Herbert's death,

[14] "Church Music," in *The Poems of George Herbert*, ed. Ernest Rhys (London: Walter Scott, 1885), 59. George Herbert (1593–1633) devoted most of his poetry to the Church of England, which he served as a rector near Salisbury. None of his poetry was published during his lifetime. Some publications refer to him as a "late orator of the University of Cambridge."

[15] Ibid., 260ff.

... he rose suddenly from his bed and couch, called for one of his instruments, took it into his hand, and said,

>My God, my God!
>My music shall find Thee,
>And every string
>Shall have his attribute to sing.

7
Music in Jacobean Prose

THE FIRST HALF of the seventeenth century in England, with its civil wars and the aggressive influence of the Puritans, offered a poor climate for fine fiction. This is not to say great numbers of works were not published, but prose by fine writers was not abundant. Although the writers we quote here make philosophical comments, they are not by real philosophers. They are rather reflections on contemporary Jacobean life, made by doctors, preachers, playwrights and writers of prose.

Jacobean Prose

SIR THOMAS BROWNE, in his "Religio Medici," reminds us of some of the ancient philosophers when he offers the personal perspective that all music has something of the divine in it.

> For there is a music wherever there is a harmony, order, or proportion; and thus far we may maintain "the music of spheres" for those well-ordered motions, and regular paces, though they give no sound unto the ear, yet to the understanding they strike a note most full of harmony. Whatsoever is harmonically composed delights in harmony, which makes me much distrust the symmetry of those heads which declaim against all church music. For myself, not only from my obedience but my particular genius I do embrace it: for even that vulgar and tavern music, which makes one man

merry, another mad, strikes in me a deep fit of devotion, and a profound contemplation of the first composer. There is something in it of divinity more than the ear discovers: it is an hieroglyphical and shadowed lesson of the whole world, and creatures of God,—such a melody to the ear, as the whole world, well understood, would afford the understanding. In brief, it is a sensible fit of that harmony which intellectually sounds in the ears of God. I will not say, with Plato, the soul is an harmony, but harmonic, and has its nearest sympathy with music ... [1]

Izaak Walton reminds his readers that one's experience as a listener has a very direct relationship with the kind of music one enjoys.

> What musick doth a pack of dogs then make to any man, whose heart and ears are so happy as to be set to the tune of such instruments?[2]

In this strict Puritan environment stories such as Noah and the Flood, and the subsequent necessity of rebuilding the human species, were taken quite seriously. Someone must have wondered, what happened to the accumulated knowledge of music before the flood? Walton offers an explanation for how the early knowledge of music survived the Flood. "Others say," he reports, that Seth, one of the sons of Adam, engraved the knowledge of mathematics and music, and the rest of previous knowledge, on pillars.[3]

Modern philologists believe that vocal music, as a form of communicating feeling, must have preceded even the most primitive of languages. It is from this perspective that our eye was drawn to Thomas Dekker's essay on lowlife in London, in which he discusses a slang speech of the underworld, of which little is known today, called *canting*. In this passage we get little more than a kind of etymology of the word.

> This word *canting* seems to be derived from the Latin verbe (*canto*) which signifies in English, to sing, or to make a sound with words, that is to say to speake. And very aptly may *canting* take his *derivatio a cantando*, from singing, because amongst these beggarly consorts that can play upon no better instruments, the language of *canting* is a kinde of musicke,

[1] *Sir Thomas Browne's Works*, ed. Simon Wilkin (London: Pickering, 1836), II, 106ff. A few pages later [Ibid., 32]. Sir Thomas Browne (1605–1682), one of the best prose writers of the period, was educated at Oxford and became a provincial doctor in Norwich.

[2] Izaak Walton, *The Compleat Angler* (London: Oxford University Press, 1935), 31. Izaak Walton (1593–1683) is best known for his biographies of contemporary English writers.

[3] Ibid., 38.

and he that in such assemblies can *cant* best, is counted the best Musician.[4]

The familiarity of the general English society with music was such that one finds in ordinary discussion an extraordinary range of musical metaphors. Consider, for example, the broad variety of such metaphors by a single writer, Thomas Dekker:

To represent the well-together person:

> ... what monsters they please to set [on] all the world and all the people in it out of tune, and the worse Musicke they make, the more sport it is for him.[5]

As a metaphor for the four winds:

> East, West, North, and South, the foure Trumpetters of the Worlde, that never blow themselves out of breath ...[6]

To describe a papal representative who tries to be all things to all people:

> He's like an Instrument of sundry strings,
> Not one in tune, yet any note he sings.[7]

To describe "cooperation" between two people:

> As strings of an instrument, though we render several sounds, yet let both our sounds cadence [*close up*] in sweet concordant Musicke.[8]

To represent the Spanish and French conspiring against the English:

> To be short, such strange mad musick doe they play upon their Sacke-buttes ...[9]

On the reader's sympathy with his writing:

> If the Notes please thee, my paines are well bestowed. If to thine ear they found untuneable, much are they not to be blamed, in regard they are the melodies [Aires] of a Sleeping Man.[10]

[4] Thomas Dekker, "Lanthorne and Candle-Light" (1609), Grosart, *The Non-Dramatic Works of Thomas Dekker* (New York, Russell & Russell, 1963), III, 194. Thomas Dekker (b. 1570) was a very fluent writer, producing plays of his own and in collaboration with others, in addition to "entertainments" and pamphlets on a variety of subjects. It has been said that no writer gave a more vivid picture of London at this time. He, however, failed to earn a living and was often in prison—once for three years. Nothing is known of him after the 1630s.

[5] Thomas Dekker, "The Divels Last Will and Testament" (1609), Ibid., III, 357.

[6] Thomas Dekker, "The Seven Deadly Sinnes of London" (1606), Ibid., II, 97

[7] Thomas Dekker, "A Papist in Armes' (1606), Ibid., II,174.

[8] Thomas Dekker, "The Dead Tearme" (1608), Ibid., IV, 71.

[9] Thomas Dekker, "The Seven Deadly Sinnes of London" (1606), Ibid., II, 44.

[10] Thomas Dekker, "Dekker his Dream," (1620), III, 12.

Other writers were equally creative in their use of music in figures of speech. Thomas Fuller, in warning the reader to beware of "boisterous and over-violent exercise," writes,

> Ringing oftentimes has made good musick on the bells, and puts mens bodies out of tune.[11]

Thomas Overbury uses music as a metaphor to characterize the duties of the lawyer, a profession associated with amateur music making in seventeenth century England.

> He knows so much in Musique, that he affects only the most and cunningest discords; rarely a perfect concord, especially sung, except in *fine*.[12]

Finally, we don't know what else it could be but a nice pun, when John Earle describes a Puritan mother who would not allow her daughters to study the virginals, "because of their affinity with organs."[13]

On the Purpose of Music

THOMAS BROWNE OFFERS, as an example of the frequently mentioned capacity of music to soothe, a strange and modern interpretation of the myth of Orpheus.

> There were a crew of mad women retired unto a mountain, from whence, being pacified by his music, they descended with boughs in their hands; which, unto the fabulosity of those times, proved a sufficient ground to celebrate unto all posterity the magic of Orpheus's harp ... [14]

Thomas Dekker also mentions this purpose of music in one passage where he writes of "Musicke charming thine ear,"[15] but in another place he refers to the absence of music to soothe those in prison.

> What musicke hath he to cheer up his Spirits in this sadness? None but this, he hears wretches (equally miserable) breaking their heart-strings every night with groans, every day with sighs, every hour with cares ... [16]

[11] Thomas Fuller, *The Holy State and the Profane State* [1642], ed. Maximilian Walten (New York: AMS Press, 1966), II, 184. Thomas Fuller (1608–1661) was a chaplain to Charles II.

[12] *The "Conceited Newes" of Sir Thomas Overbury and His Friends*, ed. James Savage (Gainesville: Scholars' Facsimiles, 1968), 119. Sir Thomas Overbury (1581–1613) was also a poet.

[13] "A She Precise Hypocrite," in John Earle, *Microcosmography* [1628] (St. Clair Shores: Scholarly Press, 1971), 73. John Earle (1600–1665) was a chaplain to Charles II, during the king's exile, and a dean of Westminster during the Restoration.

[14] *Sir Thomas Browne's Works*, II, 220.

[15] Thomas Dekker, "The Seven Deadly Sinnes of London" (1606), II, 128.

[16] Thomas Dekker, "Jests to Make you Merrie" (1607), Ibid., II, 341.

Thomas Browne is perplexed by the strange nature of dreams and points to music as a soothing means of preparing for trouble-free sleep.

> Half our days we pass in the shadow of the earth; and the brother of death exacts a third part of our lives. A good part of our sleep is peered out with visions and fantastical objects, wherein we are confessedly deceived. The day supplies us with truths; the night with fictions and falsehoods, which uncomfortably divide the natural account of our beings. And, therefore, having passed the day in sober labors and rational enquiries of truth, we are fain to betake ourselves into such a state of being, wherein the soberest heads have acted all the monstrosities of melancholy, and which unto open eyes are no better than folly and madness.
>
> Happy are they that go to bed with grand music, like Pythagoras, or have ways to compose the fantastical spirit, whose unruly wanderings take off inward sleep ... [17]

[17] *Sir Thomas Browne's Works*, IV, 355.

Another traditional purpose of music is to attract the ladies, as we see in Thomas Overbury, in a character sketch of a Lover, where he suggests the lover's education must include music. It is important to note, as well, his point here, that through music you reveal yourself, because music is a form of Truth.

> His fingers are his Orators, and he expresses much of himself upon some instrument.[18]

[18] *The "Conceited Newes" of Sir Thomas Overbury and His Friends*, 78.

We find one interesting reference to music therapy, where Sir Thomas Browne, a physician as well a writer of prose, could find no reason to question the folk legends of the use of music to cure bite of the Tarantula.

> Some doubt many have of the *tarantula*, or poisonous spider of Calabria, and that magical cure of the bite thereof by music. But since we observe that many attest it from experience; since the learned Kircherus has positively averred it, and set down the songs and tunes solemnly used for it; since some also affirm the *tarantula* itself will dance upon certain strokes, whereby they set their instruments against its poison, we shall not at all question it.[19]

[19] "Enquiries into Vulgar and Common Errors," in *Sir Thomas Browne's Works*, II, 536.

8
Entertainment Music in Baroque England

> The slight and frivolous amusements, in vogue,
> do not less hurt our taste
> and discernment of what is really good,
> than our most criminal passions.
> *William Wycherley*[1]

[1] *The Complete Works of William Wycherley* (New York: Russell & Russell, 1964), IV, 129.

WE BEGIN WITH THE MOST DISCUSSED aspect of entertainment music in Baroque England, the common street fiddler. It is ironic, in retrospect, for the Baroque Period was when all the great modern strings were being made, instruments which would raise the string family to the very top of music culture. That notwithstanding, these contemporary observations do remind the reader that before about the year 1550 the wind instrument player was the recognized professional musician and the string players generally were wandering musicians playing for hand-outs. Indeed, one of the most commonly mentioned street musicians before the Baroque was the "beer fiddler."

So common was the street fiddler in Baroque England that we have some lengthy portraits of this humble musician. One of these portraits is John Earle's, "A Poor Fiddler."

> A poor fiddler is a man and a fiddle out of case: and he in worse case than his fiddle. One that rubs two sticks together (as the Indians strike fire), and rubs a poor living out of it; partly from this, and partly from your charity, which is more

in the hearing than giving him, for he sells nothing dearer than to be gone. He is just so many strings above a beggar, though he have but two: and yet he begs too, only not in the downright "for God's sake," but with a shrugging "God bless you," and his face is more pained than the blind man's. Hunger is the greatest pain he takes, except a broken head sometimes, and the laboring *John Dory*. Otherwise his life is so many fits of mirth, and it is some mirth to see him. A good feast shall draw him five miles by the nose, and you shall track him again by the scent. His other pilgrimages are fairs and good houses, where his devotion is great to the Christmas; and no man loves good times better. He is in league with the tapsters for the worshipful of the inn, whom he torments next morning with his art, and has their names more perfect than their men. A new song is better to him than a new jacket, especially if bawdy, which he calls merry, and hates naturally the Puritan, as an enemy to this mirth. A country wedding and Whitsun ale are the two main places he domineers in, where he goes for a musician, and overlooks the bagpipe. The rest of him is drunk, and in the stocks.[2]

Thomas Dekker, known for his vivid pictures of London at his time, was especially brutal in his treatment of the vagrant fiddler. In one place he refers to "Common Juglers, Fidlers, and Players" called "Beasts,"[3] and in another place he describes a man as "his acquaintance is more cheape, than a common Fidlers."[4] In his "The Ravens Almanacke," we find another portrait:

O you common Fidlers likewise that scrape out a poore living out of dryed Cats guts: I prophesie that many of you shall this yeare be troubled with abominable noises and singing in your heads: insomuch that a great part of you shall die beggars, and those that survive shall feed upon melody for want of meat, playing by two of the clock in a frostie morning under a Window, and then be mocked with a shilling tied (through a hole) to a string, which shall be thrown to make it jingle in your ears, but presently be drawn up again, while you rake in the durst for a largesse.[5]

Dekker, in one story, alludes to professional entertainment brokers from whom one could engage musicians for the home. Here he begs not to send any more out of tune fiddlers but harps instead:

[2] John Earle, *Microcosmography* [1628] (St. Clair Shores: Scholarly Press, 1971), 38ff. John Earle (1600–1665) was a chaplain to Charles II, during the king's exile, and a dean of Westminster during the Restoration.

[3] Thomas Dekker, "The Dead Tearme" (1608), in *The Dramatic Works of Thomas Dekker,* ed. Fredson Bowers (Cambridge: University Press, 1955), IV, 55. Thomas Dekker (b. 1570) was a very fluent writer, producing plays of his own and in collaboration with others, in addition to "entertainments" and pamphlets on a variety of subjects. He, however, failed to earn a living and was often in prison—once for three years. Nothing is known of him after the 1630s.

[4] Thomas Dekker, "The Seven Deadly Sinnes of London" (1606), Ibid., II, 96.

[5] Thomas Dekker, "The Ravens Almanacke" (1609), Ibid., IV, 192ff.

May it therefore please thee (O thou pay-mistress to all the fidlers that should haunt our houses, if thou wouldest put them in tune) to send (at least) some of thy Harpers to sound their nine-penie musicke in our eares.[6]

[6] Thomas Dekker, "The Peace is Broken" (1609), Ibid.

We have yet another lengthy portrait of the fiddler, by Samuel Butler. This account, in particular, gives us also a glimpse of English humor of the day.

> A fidler commits a rape upon the ear ... He ... sets men together by the ears, enchants them with his magical rod, his fidlestic, out of themselves, and makes them skip as if they were bit with a tarantula ... He tickles their ears ... while he picks their pockets ... The roughness of his bow makes his strings speak, which otherwise would be silent and unuseful, and when he grows humorous himself, (which is not seldom) and will not play, he is used as niggedly till he does. He is an earwig, that creeps into a mans ear and torments him, until he is got out again. The scrapings of his fiddle and horse-tail (like horse-radish) with white wine and sugar, or brandy make excellent sauce for a whore. He scratches and rubs the itch of lovers upon his fiddle, to the wonderful delight of those that have catched it, till it turns to a worse disease: for his fiddlestic is but a rubber made of a horses tail to carry sinners with, and he scrubs and firks them till they kick and sling, as if the Devil were in them. The noise of cats-guts sets them a caterwauling, as those, that are bitten with a mad dog, are said to foam at the mouth and bark ... He is [welcome in] all taverns, as being as useful to relish a glass of wine as anchovies of caviar, serves like stum to help of bad wine, and conduces wonderfully to over reckoning. He is as great a provocative, as a Romance, to love, and at weddings is a prime ingredient ... He does not live but rub out, spends time while he keeps it, is very expert in his way, and has his trade at his fingers ends.[7]

[7] Samuel Butler, *Characters*, "A Fidler."

In the Jacobean drama literature one also finds many demeaning references to the poor street fiddler. In Ben Jonson's comedy, *Poetaster* (III, iv), a comment made in passing gives us a description of one of the last of the true minstrels, the now poor vagrant musician. Tucca observes,

> We must have you turn fiddler again, slave, get a bass violin at your back, and march in a tawny coat, with one sleeve, to Goose fair ...

And in Jonson's comedy, *The Silent Woman* (III, iii), Clerimont observes,

> The smell of the venison, going through the street, will invite one noise of fiddlers or other.

In Beaumont and Fletcher's *The Honest Man's Fortune* (V, i), Mountage says to a man,

> Ye have travell'd like a Fidler to make faces,
> And brought home nothing but a case of tooth-picks.

In the Beaumont and Fletcher play, *The Chances* (V, iii), a "Fidler" is hanged for robbing a mill.

The Jacobean playwright who seemed most interested in these street musicians was Thomas Dekker, although he too treats them with contempt, as we see in his *The Whore of Babylon* (II, ii), when Campeius observes,

> Like common Fidlers, drawing down others meate
> With lickorish tunes, whilst they on scraps do eate.

A more extended dialogue is found in his *Westward Ho* (V, i), where Frank Monopoly, a nephew to the Earle, complains that the fiddlers have not begun to play, especially since the ladies have arrived.

> MONOPOLY. Why Chamberlin? will not these Fidlers be drawn forth? are they not in tune yet? Or are the Rogues afraideth Statute, and dare not travel so far without a passport? ...
>
> *[Enter Chamberlin]*
>
> CHAMBERLIN. Anon sir, here sir, at hand sir.
> MONOPOLY. Where's this noise? what a lowsie Townes this? Has *Brainford* no musick in it.
> CHAMBERLIN. The are but rozining sir, and they will scrape themselves into your company presently.
> MONOPOLY. Plague on their Cats guts, and their scraping: dost not see women here, and can we thinkst thou be without a noise then?
> CHAMBERLIN. The truth is sir, one of the poor instrument caught a sore mischance last night: his most base bridge fell down, and belike they are making a gathering for the reparations of that.
> WHIRLEPOOLE. When they come, lets have em with a pox.

In *If This be not a Good Play* (II, i) we find an extraordinary account of no fewer than one hundred and twenty street musicians, most of whom seem to be string players. Since they also are foreign speaking, one is tempted to wonder if the audience took this as a satirical reference to the French "24 Violins of the king," a tradition which made its way to London during the seventeenth century.

> BRISCO. Without now waits
>   Musicke in some ten languages: each one sweares
>   (By *Orpheus* fiddle-case) they will tickle your eares
>   If they can't do it with scraping.
> NARCISSO. Theres seven score Noise at least of English fidlers.
> IOUINELLI. Seven score! they are able to eate up a city in very scraps.
> BRISCO. Very base-viol men most of them: besides whole swarmes of Welsh harpes, Irish bagpipes, Jewes trompes, and French kitts.
>   All these made I together play:
>   But their damned catter-wralling,
>   Frightened me away.

Finally, in *The Witch of Edmonton* (III, iv), Dekker gives us a poor fiddler, known as "Sawgut," who finds his instrument makes no sound and he laments,

> I'll lay mine Ear to my Instrument, that my poor Fiddle is bewitch'd. I play'd "The Flowers in May," even now, as sweet as a Violet; now 'twill not go against the hair: you see I can make no more Musick than a Beetle of a Cow-turd.

With the arrival of the popular public journals during the late Baroque one still finds unkind references to the street fiddlers. By this time London would have known real artist performers on the modern strings, but it would seem their brothers were still playing for hand-outs. In the *Tatler* for August 18, 1709, for example, the fiddler is listed together with "Pimps, Footmen and Lackeys" and the issue for February 26, 1712, mentions "some Fiddles heard in the Street..."

We also note one reference to a barber-fiddler, an occupation in earlier times associated with the guitar. The *Spectator* for July 30, 1712, mentions a barber whose fiddle was broken.

We will continue with the observations on the musical entertainments of the lower class, in particular with the association with drink and taverns so characteristic of the "beer fiddler" discussed above. Ben Johnson, in his play, *The Staple of News* (III, ii), even suggests that at a banquet not a drop of wine could be poured without music.

> Your meat should be served in with curious dances,
> And set upon the board with virgin hands,
> Tuned to their voices; not a dish removed,
> But to the music, nor a drop of wine
> Mixed with his water without harmony.

Similarly, in Otway's Restoration play, *Friendship in Fashion* (II, line 266), we read, that "Musick is as great an encouragement to drinking, as fighting."[8] In the journals of the late Baroque there are also occasional comments on the entertainment venues of the lower classes. Typical among these are the *Spectator* for May 23, 1711, which mentions the singing of Catches "at all Hours" alternating with drinking and smoking in a tavern and the issue for July 21, 1712, in which Steele mentions visiting an entertainment of "the lower Order of Britons" at the Bear-Garden, where he heard, among other things, a performance by two disabled drummers.[9]

[8] Additional drinking songs can be found in Vanbrugh's *The Provoked Wife* (III, ii); George Etherege's *The Man of Mode* (IV, i); and his *She Would if she could* (IV, ii), where the two singers are both drunk.

[9] The *Spectator* for April 30, 1712, discusses Lapland and mentions, unfortunately without detail, "the famous stories of their drums."

In the diary of Samuel Pepys there are a number of references to a variety of popular entertainment forms, heard in the taverns and in the streets. Of these, the ones of most interest to us are the descriptions of amateur multi-part popular singing. His diary records on November 9, 1663, for example, his hearing impromptu singing in a tavern "in three parts very finely." On July 27, 1663, while out for a walk, he reports coming across, under some trees,

> some Citizens, met by chance, that sing four or five parts excellently. I have not been more pleased with a snapp of Musique, considering the circumstances of the time and place, in all my life anything so pleasant.

An entry for April 17, 1668, describing popular singing in the grotto of a tavern, in which Pepys found "admirable pleasure," may also have been part-songs.

The street singer, along with the beer fiddler, was the subject of the most commentary in Baroque English literature. John Gay has written a poem describing an itinerant fiddler and singer named Bowzybeus,[10] whom we first find asleep from drink.

[10] "Saturday; or, the Flights," in *The Works of John Gay* (London: Edward Jeffery, 1745), II, 116ff. John Gay (1685–1732) was born of humble stock and worked for a while as a silk merchant. He became one of the most beloved of English literary figures.

> When fast asleep they Bowzybeus spied,
> His hat and oaken staff lay close beside.
> That Bowzybeus who could sweetly sing,
> Or with the rosined bow torment the string:
> That Bowzybeus who with fingers speed
> Could call soft warblings from the breathing reed;
> That Bowzybeus who with jocund tongue,
> Ballads and roundelays and catches sung ...

Folks passing by awaken him and plea for some songs:

> No sooner began he raise his tuneful song,
> But lads and lasses round about him throng.
> No ballad-singer placed above the crown
> Sings with a note so shrilling sweet and loud,
> No parish-clerk who calls the psalm so clear,
> Like Bowzybeus soothes the attentive ear.

Bowzybeus sings a very wide variety of songs, beginning with songs about nature, followed by songs describing "fairs and shows." Among these songs are "Jack Pudding," "Rare shews" and songs about Punch, but one is quite different,

> Then sad he sung *The Children in the Wood*.
> Ah barbarous uncle, stained with infant blood!

Next he turns to songs of war.

> To louder strains he raised his voice, to tell
> What woeful wars in *Chevy-chase* befell,
> When *Piercy* drove the deer with hound and horn,
> Wars to be wept by children yet unborn!

Now he sings more songs of England, and then,

> Then he was seized with a religious qualm,
> And of a sudden sung the hundredth psalm.

He finally finished singing and "as he reels along," goes on his way, still drunk!

The reader will notice in his account that we are given the titles of actual popular songs. Such information is actually not rare. In a poem by Alexander Pope, "Imitations of Horace," he writes of the public interrupting plays by crying for popular tunes, in this case "The Coal-black Joke," an indecent song in a ballad opera, *The Beggar's Wedding*.

> The many-headed monster of the pit;
> A senseless, worthless, and unhonored crowd;
> Who, to disturb their betters mighty proud,
> Clattering their sticks before ten lines are spoke,
> Call for the farce, the bear, or the black-joke.[11]

[11] "Imitations of Horace," Book II, Epistle I, lines 305ff, in Ibid., III, 367.

In the *Spectator* for November 26, 1711, we find mention of beggars singing a song called, "The Merry Beggars."

The Jacobean poet, George Wither, makes a passing reference to genuine popular music.

> I might have brought some other things to pass,
> Made Fiddlers Songs, or Ballads, like an Ass.[12]

[12] *Works of George Wither* (New York: Franklin, 1967), Spenser Society, Nr. 10, "A Satyre," 439. George Wither (1588–1667), one of the so-called Cavalier Poets was an officer in the Puritan army and most of his poetry is political in nature.

Of particular interest is his reference here to the singers of the large body of broadside ballads, the words for many of which are extant from the seventeenth century. These were published in the form of poetry, without the music, and the universal understanding today is that they were all sung to known popular tunes. Scholars do not want to think of these ballads as *real* poetry, for they were written by hired professional rhyme-makers to serve as a kind of journalism. And they seem to us more a kind of public information form of journalism, than music. Who, we wonder, would stand around and *sing* a ballad with the title, "Strange and Dreadful News from Holland or The Sad Account of a Fearful Storm" (November, 1686), or "The Manifestation of Joy upon the Publication of His Majesty's Declaration Allowing Liberty of Conscience" (April 4, 1687).

Whatever we call them, they are certainly mirrors of ordinary life and it is for this reason that we regret that the lyrics of these ballads so rarely offer insights on musical practice. Generally one only finds an occasional familiar metaphor, such as the trumpet of the Day of Judgment, or a reference to the trumpets and drums of war. Nevertheless, we will quote a few lines to indicate the general level. In "A Warning for all Good Fellows to Take Heed of Punks Enticements," we find musicians enticing persons to the tavern.

> Bagpipers and Fidlers,
> With Phife playing Drummers:[13]
> With Musicke will merry be,
> To welcome all commers:
> That unto such places lewd,
> Often repair:
> Yet hath them and sing with me,
> Come no more there.[14]

Contemporary evaluation of this material was mixed. While Butler associated these ballad singers with "Cat-purse" and "Orange-Women,"[15] some writers highly valued this form of folk music. William Shenstone writes,

> There is nothing give me greater pleasure than the simplicity of style & sentiment that is observable in old English ballads.[16]

> ......

> The ways of ballad-singers, and the cries of halfpenny pamphlets, appeared so extremely humorous, from my lodgings in Fleet-street, that it gave me pain to observe them without a companion to partake.[17]

The poet Thomas Gray was sent some ballads by a friend and his response is particularly interesting.

> I have got the old Ballad ... it is in my eyes a miracle not only of ancient simplicity, but of ancient art. The great rules of Aristotle & Horace are observed in it by a writer, who perhaps had never heard their names.[18]

We also notice that ballad singing is mentioned in Defoe's *Journal of the Plague Year*, [1664–1665], where he quotes a civic order relative to keeping the citizens indoors.

[13] The fife and drum players, one-man bands of the Middle Ages.

[14] *The Pepys Ballads* (Cambridge: Harvard University Press, 1929), I, 263.

[15] Samuel Butler, *Characters*, "A Jugler." He refers to pick-pockets and venders at plays.

[16] Letter to Thomas Percy, January 4, 1758, in *Letters of William Shenstone* (Minneapolis: University of Minnesota Press, 1939), 345.

[17] William Shenstone, *Men and Manners*, 35.

[18] Letter to Edward Bedingfield, October 31, 1757, *Correspondence of Thomas Gray* (Oxford, Clarendon Press, 1971). Thomas Gray (1716–1771) spent the greater part of his adult life in academic seclusion in Cambridge.

> All plays, bear-baitings, games, singing of ballads, buckler-play, or such-like causes of assemblies of people be utterly prohibited ... [19]

While most references to street music in Baroque English literature are dismissive, a comment by a preacher reminds us that in the drab London winters, in a time when there was no recorded music, the presence of music may have been welcomed by many citizens. John Donne, in a sermon, speaks of "that good custom in these cities, [where] you hear cheerful street musick in the winter mornings."[20]

Before leaving the lower class, there is one more reference which is quite interesting. A familiar term in the literature of this period is the "music-meeting," which is taken to be a private chamber music session, if not an actual concert. On the basis of a line in Congreve's play, *The Way of the World* (V, i), one wonders if these were sometimes concerts organized specifically as entertainment events for the lower class. In this passage an association made with "singing and dancing, and such debaucheries; going to filthy plays," etc., includes,

> and profane Musick-meetings, where the lewd Trebles squeak nothing but Bawdy, and the Basses roar Blasphemy.

In the dramatic literature, poems and journals there is not as much discussion of the entertainment music of the upper class, no doubt because it was more familiar to readers. We get a small view of the long, dull hours of the upper class for which constant entertainment was needed in Chapman's play, *All Fools* (V, ii). Here, young courtiers are sitting around and in the mood for entertainment. Valerio suggests,

> Come on, lets varie our sweet time
> With sundry exercises. Boy. Tobacco.
> And Drawer, you must get us musique too,
> Call us in a cleanly noyse ...

In contrast to the beer fiddler, in upper class accounts one finds occasional reference to the modern strings. We see this in a work by Dekker, where he uses the term anciently reserved for the wind band, "Loud music," but now he

---

[19] Daniel Defoe, *A Journal of the Plague Year*, (Garden City: Doubleday, n.d.), 51. Daniel Defoe (1660–1731), a staunch Presbyterian, was the son of a London butcher and spent some years in that trade himself. Eventually he produced hundreds of literary works, while on the side serving as a spy.

[20] John Donne, "A Sermon Preached at White-hall, February 29, 1628," in *Selected Prose*, ed. Helen Gardner (Oxford: Clarendon Press, 1967), 328. John Donne (1573–1631) studied at both Oxford and Cambridge, but as a born Catholic was not permitted to receive a degree. After various attempts at professions brought him to poverty, he converted to the official Church, became famous for his sermons and eventually became dean of St. Paul's.

seems to understand the term to encompass instrumental music in general, including strings,[21] as in this description of an ensemble accompanying a boy singer.

[21] See also Dekker, *Westward Ho* (V, ii) where a stage direction reads, "Enter a noyse of Fidlers."

> His Majestie, being ready to go one, did most graciously feed the eyes of beholders with his presence, till a Song was spent: which to a loude and excellent Musicke (composed of Violins and other rare Artificiall Instruments) ...

The Renaissance viols are also mentioned relative to a pageant involving the nine Muses.

> And being come near to the Arbor, they gave a sign with a short flourish from all their Cornets, that his Majestie was at hand: whose princely eye whilest it was delighting itself with the quaint object before it, a sweet pleasure likewise courted his ear in the shape of Musicke, sent from the voices of nine Boys (all of them Queristers of St. Paul's) who in that place presenting the nine *Muses* sang the verse following to their Viols and other Instruments.

One still finds the traditional allegorical entertainment productions of the nobles which were familiar in the Renaissance. The playwright, John Marston, was involved in the creation of the "Entertainment of Alice, Dowager-countess of Derby," given for her arrival at Ashby.[22] When her Ladyship approached the park around the house "a full noise of cornets winded" and as she entered the park "treble cornets reported one to another, as giving warning of her Honor's nearer approach." As she entered the house "a consort softly played," while a speaker greeted her with poetry.

[22] Most of the text for the speakers and songs are quoted in A. H. Bullen, *The Works of John Marston* (London: Nimmo, 1887), III, 387ff.

Within the house a masque was given, its songs alternating with consorts of oboes and cornets. In a typical song, we hear the allegorical character, Ariadne, sing,

> Music and gentle night,
> Beauty, youth's chief delight,
> Pleasures all full invite
> Your due attendance to this glorious room;
> Then, if you have or wit or virtue, come,
> Oh, come! oh, come!

The first mention of string instruments is when the "violins played a new measure," to which the masquers danced.

After some more songs, there were additional dances, "measures, galliards, corantos, and levaltos."[23]

As in the above case, dance music in the theater repertoire is almost invariably associated with violins. It is because this was a familiar association it lent itself to humor, as is found in Wycherley's play, *The Gentleman Dancing-master* (IV, i), where a dancing-master winds the strings so tightly they break, so it won't be discovered that he cannot play the violin.

The only real exceptions in the dramatic literature to violin dance music are found in the plays of Behn. *The Widow Ranter* (II, ii), which is set in Virginia, calls for a dance for which only a bagpipe player is available. In *The Emperor of the Moon* (I, iii) there is a dance to a "Flute Doux."

There is a nice description of entertainment in Farquhar's Comedy, *Love and a Bottle* (II, ii). Mockmode, a young man newly graduated from the university, brags of the music he can play on his violin, even though he knows nothing about his repertoire, the titles of which are expressed in the old academic manner of the solfege abbreviations used to identify early music. The reference to the Music of the Spheres here suggests this was still a topic known to the public.[24]

> MOCKMODE. I can play the *Bells* and *Maiden Fair* already. *Alamire, Bifabemi, Cesolfa, Delasol, Ela, Effaut, Gesolrent.* I have them all by heart already. But I have been plaguily puzzled about the etymology of these notes; and certainly a man cannot arrive at any perfection, unless he understands the derivation of the terms.
> RIGADOON. [a dancing master] O Lord, Sir! That's easy. *Effaut* and *Gesolrent* were two famous *German* musicians, and the rest were *Italians*.
> MOCKMODE. But why are they only seven?
> RIGADOON. From a prodigious great bass-viol with seven strings, that played a Jig called the *Musick of the Spheres*: The seven Planets were nothing but fiddle-strings.

Regarding the educated class, judging by the popular journals of the late Baroque in England, the most conspicuous amateur musicians were lawyers. An anonymous letter to the

[23] The written text for Entertainments by Thomas Middleton are given in *The Works of Thomas Middleton* (New York: AMS Press, 1964), VII: "The Magnificent Entertainment for King James" (1603); "The Cities Love. An entertainment by water, at Chelsey and White-hall" (1616); "The Tryumphs of Honor and Industry" (1617); "The Triumphs of Love and Antiquity" (1619); "The Sun in Aries" (1621); "The Triumphs of Honor and Virtue" (1622); "The Triumphs of Integrity" (1623); "The Triumphs of Health and Prosperity" (1626). Also see *The Dramatic Works of Thomas Heywood* (New York: Russell & Russell, 1964), IV, "Londons Ius Honorarium," "Londons Sinus Salutis," and "Londini Speculum"; V, "The Port of Piety" and "Londons Peaceable Estate."

[24] Farquhar mentions the Music of the Spheres again in *The Inconstant* (IV, iii).

editor of the *Tatler*, for March 4, 1710, complains that lawyers drink all morning and engage in singing to the dulcimer and violin late at night. Addison adds that he knew two law students who had studied the oboe and concludes by recommending a civic law ordering that "no Retainers to the Law, with Dulcimer, Violin, or any other Instrument, in any Tavern within a Furlong of the Inns of Court, shall sing any Tune, or pretended Tune whatsoever." Another complaint is made about lawyers who study the oboe and are "proficients in Wind-Musick," in the *Spectator* for August 16, 1711. Steele, in the *Spectator* for January 16, 1712, presents a fictitious letter by a mistress to a lawyer:

> This man makes on the violin a certain jiggish noise to which I dance, and when that is over I sing to him some loose Air that has more wantonness than Musick in it.

In Congreve's play, *Squire Trelooby* (II, xi), it is because of the frequent association of lawyers engaging musicians that we find a song sung by two musicians disguised as lawyers.

William Shenstone, in a discussion of Vanity, has left a sad portrait of a humble bagpipe player who was a frequent source of entertainment at one of the London clubs where the upper class entertained themselves.

> I remember a bagpiper, whose physiognomy was so remarkable and familiar to a club he attended, that it was agreed to have his picture placed over their chimney-piece. There was this remarkable in the fellow, that he chose always to go barefoot, though he was daily offered a pair of shoes. However, when the painter had been so exact as to omit this little piece of dress, the fellow offered all he had in the world, the whole produce of three nights harmony, to have those feet covered in the effigy, which he so much scorned to cover in the original. Perhaps he thought it a disgrace to his instrument to be eternalized in the hands of so much apparent poverty.[25]

The dramatic literature continues the tradition found in Shakespeare of assigning to the oboe consort the music for upper class banquets. We see this in Thomas Dekker's "The Magnificent Entertainment Given to King James," a major allegorical work associated with the arrival of James I for

[25] William Shenstone, *Men and Manners* (Boston: Houghton Mifflin, 1927), 13. William Shenstone (1714–1763) attended Oxford, but did not finish. He was one of the minor figures in English literature of the early eighteenth century, but was possessed of a perceptive intelligence.

his coronation in 1603.[26] Among the interesting references to music, there was a banquet with music by "The Wayts and Haultboyes of London."

Similarly, in Beaumont and Fletcher's *The Tragedy of Valentinian* (V, viii), as Maximus and Eudoxia enter in state, the stage direction reads,

> *A Synnet with Trumpets.*
> *With a Banket prepared, with Hoboies, Musick, Song*

And again in Beaumont and Fletcher's *The Maids Tragedy* (IV) a stage direction reads,

> *Banquet. Enter King, Calianax. Hoboyes play within.*

When there were royal guests, the trumpets often performed their memorized works before the banquet table. It was perhaps with this in mind, in Beaumont and Fletcher's play, *Wit Without Money* (V, i), in preparation for a banquet, that Valentine cries out, "let me have forty Trumpets."

A curious exception to this tradition is found in Otway's play, *The Cheats of Scapin* (III, lines 340ff); for example, an order is given to hire casual musicians for a dinner.

> Then did you hear, send out and muster up all the Fidlers, (Blind or not Blind, Drunk or Sober) in the Town; let not so much as the Roaster of Tunes, with his cracked Cymbal in a Case, escape ye.

In the homes of the rising middle-class businessmen, a perhaps more modest meal replaced the banquet of the noble, but featured a performance by the host's daughter. In Beaumont and Fletcher's *The Humourous Lieutenant* (I, i) a common citizen inviting gentlemen and ladies to his home for a meal promises music and a performance by his daughter.

> Some Musick I'le assure you too,
> My toy, Sir, can play o'th' Virginals.

---

[26] The entire text is quoted in *The Dramatic Works of Thomas Dekker*, ed. Fredson Bowers (Cambridge: University Press, 1955), II, 253. A contemporary notes that not everything written was actually used on the occasion. In Ibid., III, 227ff, the text, with lyrics for songs, is given for a "Triumph" as part of the Lord Mayor Procession of 1612; in Ibid., IV, 812ff is the text for a Pageant given in 1628 for the inauguration of Richard Deane as Mayor of London, the music of which features primarily cornett consorts.

9
Military Music in the English Baroque

> The spirit-stirring drum, the ear-piercing fife,
> The royal banner, and all quality,
> Pride, pomp, and circumstance of glorious war!
> Shakespeare, *Othello*, III, iii

THE ABOVE LINES, first spoken by Othello in 1604, describe the English military music as it would remain for most of the seventeenth century. Of these instruments it was the drum which presumably had the principal responsibility for the control of the movement of the troops though its rudimentary signals. The success of this system depended upon the ability of the drummers to produce clear and unvaried signals and upon the soldiers to recognize them. If the drummers were tempted, out of boredom or musical sensitivity, to ornament or improvise on the basic signals there was a danger that the troops might not recognize the commands their leaders were sending out through the drums. This apparently had been a problem, for in 1610 a royal edict was published forbidding any variation in the performance of the military signals.

> Whereas the ancient custome of nations hath ever bene to use one certaine and constant forme of March in the warres, whereby to be distinguished one from another. And the March of this our nation, so famous in all the honourable achievements and glorious warres of this our kingdom in forraigne parts (being by the approbation of strangers themselves confest and acknowledged the best of all marches) was

through the negligence and carelessness of drummers, and by long discontinuance so altered and changed from the ancient gravity and majestie thereof, as it was in danger utterly to have bene lost and forgotten ...

Willing and commanding all drummers within our kingdome of England and principalitie of Wales exactly and precisely to observe the same, as well in this our kingdome, as abroad in the service of any forraigne prince or state, without any addition or alteration whatsoever. To the end that so ancient, famous, and commendable a custome may be preserved as a patterne and precedent to all posterite ...[1]

[1] Walpole, *Catalogue of Royal and Noble Authors*.

As mentioned above, the success of this system required the ordinary soldier to be able to learn and remember the basic drum signals. As one early writer famously observed, "It is to the voice of the Drum the Souldier should wholly attend, and not to the [melody] of the whistle."[2] To this end, the Earl of Arundel and Surrey issued an edict in 1639 stating,

[2] Markham, *Five Decades of Epistles of Warre* (1622).

Every soldier shall diligently observe and learn the distinct and different sounds of Drums, Fifes, and Trumpets, that he may know to answer and obey each of them in time of service.[3]

[3] *Lawes and Ordinances of Warre*, quoted in Grove, *Dictionary of Music* (1980), XII, 316.

But even allowing for the soldier to ignore the "melody of the fife," a rather well-trained ear would have still been necessary if the soldier were to be able to distinguish among the long list of military drum signals given by Markham.

First in the morning the discharge or breaking up of the *Watch*, then a preparation or Summons to make them repair to their colours; then a beating away before they begin to march; after that a *March* according to the nature and custom of the country (for diuers countries have diuers Marches), then a *Charge*, then a *Retrait*, then a *Troupe*, and lastly a *Battalion* or a *Battery*, besides other sounds which depending on the phantasttikenes of forain nations are not so useful.[4]

[4] Markham, "Of Drummes and Phiphes," in *Five Decades of Epistles of Warre*, I, v.

One would judge that the recognition of these signals had become quite second nature, judging by a comment in Otway's play, *The Souldiers Fortune* (I, lines 300ff), where a character compares whores who ply their trade on "automatic pilot" to "an old soldier that understands all his exercise by beat of Drum."

We notice in Samuel Pepys' *Diary* that even a civilian noticed when a drum cadence seemed inappropriate.

> Here in the streets I did hear the Scotch march beat by the drums before the soldiers, which is very odd.[5]

[5] Pepys Diary, June 30, 1667.

Perhaps even this was not so unusual for it would have been the assumption of the general public's familiarity which would have made possible a song which imitates a drum in Nathaniel Lee's play, *Sophonisba* (IV, i):

> Hark, hark, the Drums rattle,
> Dub a dub to the Battle.
> Tararara, Tararara the Trumpets too tattle,
> Now, now they come on, and pell mell they mingle.

This same assumed familiarity of the public for these drum signals would have been necessary for a lengthy humorous passage regarding a specific drum signal, the "Granadeer-March," in the epilogue of George Farquhar's play, *The Recruiting Officer*.

> All ladies and gentlemen, that are willing to see the Comedy called the *Recruiting Officer*, let them repair tomorrow night by six a clock to the sign of the Theater Royal in Drury Lane and they shall be kindly entertained—
>
> We scorn the vulgar Ways to bid you come,
> Whole Europe now obeys the Call of Drum.
> The Soldier, not the Poet, here appears,
> And beats up for a Corps of Volunteers:
> He finds that Musick chiefly does delight ye,
> And therefore chooses Musick to invite ye.
>
> Beat the Granadeer March—Row, row, tow—Gentlemen, this piece of Musick, called an *Overture to a Battel*, was composed by a famous *Italian* Master, and was performed with wonderful success, at the great Operas of *Vigo*, *Schellenberg*, and *Blenheim*; it came off with the applause of all Europe, excepting *France*; the *French* found it a little too rough for their *Delicatesse*.

> Some that have acted on those glorious stages,
> Are here to witness to succeeding Ages,
> That no Musick like the Granadeer's engages.

> Ladies, we must admit that this Musick of ours is not altogether so soft as *Bonancini's*, yet we dare affirm, that it has laid more people asleep than all the *Camilla's* in the world; and you'll condescend to own, that it keeps one awake, better than any *Opera* that ever was acted.

> The Granadeer March seems to be a composure excellently adapted to the genius of the *English*; for no Musick was ever followed so far by us, nor with so much alacrity; and with all deference to the present subscription, we must say that the Granadeer March has been subscribed for by the whole Grand Alliance; and we presume to inform the ladies that it always has the pre-eminence abroad, and is constantly heard by the tallest, handsomest men in the whole army.

But, familiarity can lead to contempt. In Beaumont and Fletcher's play, *The Humourous Lieutenant* (I, ii), a stage direction reads "Drums a March," but Celia is not impressed.

> Pox on these bawling Drums.

Later (II, iv) even the lieutenant exhibits no love of the military drums.

> I hate all noises too,
> Especially the noise of Drums ...

We might also mention here that a comment in Samuel Pepys' *Diary* for February 3, 1661, is taken by some scholars as an indication that the expanded percussion associated with "Turkish Music" had arrived in London:

> So to White-hall, where I stayed to hear the trumpets and kettle-drums—and then the other drums; which is much cried up, though I think it dull, vulgar music.

The drummer, because of this responsibility and because he was a noncombatant, led a contemporary writer to observe that he should be considered,

> rather a man of peace than of the sword, and it is most dishonorable in any man wittingly and out of knowledge to strike him or wound him.[6]

[6] Markham, quoted in Henry Farmer, *Military Music* (London, 1912), 40.

Further responsibilities led to the establishment of the position of "Drum-major." Among these responsibilities, other than being a man "of great perfection in his science,"[7] were seeing to the provisions of the drums and fifes [dromes and phifes],[8] the discipline of these players ("with his staff correct the drums which fail in their duty"[9]) and "likewise be well skilled in several languages and tongues."[10]

The trumpeter was also carefully chosen and, according to Elton, must be "a politic, discreet and cunning person."[11] Sir James Turner adds,

> The trumpeter should be witty and discreet, and must drink little, so that he may be rather apt to circumvent others, rather than be circumvented; he should be cunning, and wherever his is sent, he should ... observe warily the works, guards, and sentinels of an enemy, and give an account of them.[12]

A publication of 1635 says the trumpeter was given a sword, but with a broken point—to demonstrate that he was a noncombatant.[13] The seventeenth century military treatise by Markham lists the common English trumpet signals, with their ancient Italian and French names:

> The first point of Warre is *Butte sella*, clap on your saddles; *Mounte Cauallo*, mount on horseback; *Tucquet*, march; *Carga, carga*, an Alarme to charge; *A la Standardo*, a retrait, or retire to your colours; *Auquet*, to the Watch, or a discharge for the watch, besides diuers other points, as Proclamations, Cals, Summons, all which are most necessary for euery Souldier both to know.[14]

Quite apart from the functional use of these military signals relative to movement on the battle field was an accompanying psychological fear raised in the listener because of the association of these signals with battle. Even the Puritan, John Bunyan, points to this in his "The Holy War," where he describes a drummer who served under Lord Lucifer and the Diabolonians.

> This, to speak truth, was amazingly hideous to hear; it frightened all men seven miles round, if they were but awake and heard it.[15]

---

[7] Thomas Digges, *An Arithmetical Warlike Treatise* (London, 1590).

[8] Gerat Barry, *A Discourse of Military Discipline* (Brussels, 1634).

[9] Du Praissac, *The Art of Warre* (Cambridge, 1639).

[10] Richard Elton, *The Compleat Body of the Art Military* (London, 1650).

[11] Ibid.

[12] Sir James Turner, *Pallas Armata* (1683).

[13] *Souldier's Accidence*, quoted in Farmer, *Military Music*, 40.

[14] Markham, *Five Decades of Epistles of Warre*, III, i.

[15] "The Holy War," in *The Works of John Bunyan*, ed. George Offor (London: Blackie and Son, 1853), III, 342, 347. John Bunyan (1628–1688) is considered the greatest prose writer among the Puritans of the seventeenth century. Only the Bible was so widely read in English homes for the subsequent three centuries. Bunyan was also the epitome of the "hell and brimstone" preacher.

Later the drummer gives various signals and again the observation is made, "no noise was ever heard upon earth more terrible."

We find a reference to this again in Beaumont and Fletcher's play, *The Martial Maid* (V, iii) when, after the stage direction calls for "Drums within," Sayavedra observes,

> Hark their Drums speak their insatiate thirst
> Of blood, and stop their ears against pious peace ...

Similarly, in Sedley's Restoration play, *Antony and Cleopatra* (II, i), after a stage direction "A noise of Drums," we find,

> You hear how Drums and Trumpets fill the Air,
> And for a scene of blood our minds prepare.

In Dryden's play, *King Arthur* (III, ii), Emmeline, when she thinks the battle is over, makes a rather dark reference to the trumpet's association with the military.

> Are all those trumpets dead themselves, at last,
> That used to kill men with their thundering sounds?

But there was another side to this coin. From the most ancient times it had been recognized that these signals also had the ability to inspire and warm the hearts of the soldier. We see this in the character, Lyndaraxa, in Dryden's play, *The Conquest of Granada*, where following a stage direction indicating the sounding of an alarm (III, i) we find contrasting reactions,

> ALMAHIDE. The noise my soul does through my senses wound.
> LYNDARAXA. Methinks it is a noble, sprightly sound,
>   The trumpet's clangor, and the clash of arm!
>   This noise may chill your blood, but mine it warms.

We see this again in Emmeline's comment, in Dryden's play, *King Arthur* (I, ii), as the men leave for battle:

> But lead me nearer to the trumpet's face;
> For that brave sound upholds my fainting heart.

Two examples from Restoration poetry can be seen in a work by Edward Young, who writes of this with respect to the percussion,

> How the drums all around
> Soul-rousing resound![16]

and in a work by Matthew Prior.

> While then your Hero drowns his rising fear
> With Drums Alarms and Trumpets Sounds.[17]

As in the case of the public familiarity of the drum signals, the use of the trumpets must have also had some level of recognition. Dryden explains in his play, *The Conquest of Granada*, that he uses these instruments on stage in order to provide verisimilitude for the plays themselves.

> To those who object my frequent use of drums and trumpets ... I answer [it is a long tradition on the English stage] ... But, I add further, that these warlike instruments, and even their presentation of fighting on the stage, are no more than necessary to produce the effects of an heroic play; that is, to raise the imagination of the audience, and to persuade them, for the time, that what they behold in the theater is really performed. The poet is then to endeavor an absolute dominion over the minds of the spectators.[18]

There is a suggestion in Samuel Pepys' *Diary* that the public's recognition of the king's trumpets made for easy identification of the king's presence. When he sees the king accompanied by his "Kettledrums and Trumpets," going to the Exchange to lay the corner-stone for a new building in 1667,[19] he may have recalled a conversation the previous year with a French visitor on the subject of Louis XIV.[20] He is told that when the king goes to see his mistress, Madame La Valière, he goes with this trumpets and timpani, who "stay before the house while he is with her." In Dryden's play, *The Spanish Fryar* (I, i), there is a similar instance of a trumpet signal for recognition of a general.

> I hear the General's Trumpets: Stand, and mark
> How he will be received; I fear, but coldly ...

In this same playwright's *Oedipus* (I, i) and in Act IV, scene i, a trumpet sounds for the purpose of identifying the native country of a character.

---

[16] Edward Young, "The Best Argument for Peace," in *Edward Young: The Complete Works* (Hildesheim: Olms, 1968), II, 57.

[17] "An Ode in Imitation of Horace," in *The Literary Works of Matthew Prior* (Oxford: Clarendon, 1959), I, 117. Matthew Prior (1664–1721) was a friend of Gay and Swift and liked to call himself "only a poet by accident."

[18] *The Works of John Dryden*, ed. Walter Scott (London: William Miller, 1808), IV, 22ff.

[19] Pepys *Diary*, October 23, 1667.

[20] Ibid., June 19, 1663.

Because of the familiarity of the military instruments with the public, the civic officials could call upon them in an emergency to help control the public, as we see in Pepys' *Diary* in the case of a public protest over some citizens put in a pillory for beating their master,

> ... drums all up and down the city was beat to raise the train-bands for to quiet the town.[21]

[21] Ibid., March 26, 1664.

and in another case to alert the citizens to a fire:

> Drums beat and trumpets, and the guards everywhere spread—running up and down in the street.[22]

[22] Ibid., November 9, 1666.

With the restoration of the monarchy in 1660, the timpani begins to appear as a member of the trumpet corps, first in the royal Life Guard. These players were paid somewhat better, due to their association with the king, and were given silver trumpets and velvet coats, trimmed with silk and silver lace and embroidered with the royal arms.[23] In the early years of the eighteenth century the artillery units were allowed to have timpani and rather than carry them on horses they constructed special wagons for the purpose. A curious order during the Flanders Campaign of 1747 required the timpani players to "mount the kettledrum carriage" and play all night long—presumably to make the enemy think the artillery was still firing.[24]

[23] Farmer, *Military Music*, 38.

The bagpipe, an instrument with ancient ties to nobles, also makes a reappearance during the seventeenth century. A document of 1683 suggests it returned with its reputation not quite in place.

[24] One of the few extant letters by Handel is one of February 24, 1750, requesting the loan of the "Artillery Kettle Drums for use in the Oratorio's in this season."

> In some places a piper is allowed to each company: the *Germans* have him, and I look upon their pipe as a warlike instrument. The bagpipe is good enough musick for them who love it; but sure it is not so good as the Almain Whistle. With us any captain may keep a piper in his company, and maintain him too, for no pay is allowed him, perhaps just as much as he dererveth.[25]

[25] Turner, quoted in Farmer, *Military Music*, 28.

As with the other European countries, it was the arrival of the Hautboisten band which represented a major turning point in English military music. The military version of the Hautboisten band appears in 1678, together with the creation of the new Horse Grenadiers, and consisted of four oboes and two bassoons.[26] These bands, of course, played music and not mere signals and therefore their popularity rapidly spread. According to Farmer, who was unfamiliar with the tradition of doubling, these bands never numbered more than six players,[27] although Panoff claims that twelve was standard by 1685.[28]

Following the general economic conditions of the court in the latter part of the seventeenth century, there appears to have been a retrenchment in the size of these military bands, indeed we can see in an order of 1731 which informed the Grenadier Company of the Honorable Artillery Company of London that they might have "one curtail three hautboys and no more!"[29]

The oboe and bassoon players had to be recruited from the civilian world, rather than within the military, and it appears the Drum-major and Sergeant-trumpeter had the authority to "impress," which is to say kidnap, musicians for this purpose. A report survives of a Mr. John Digges who had challenged a Sergeant-trumpeter to a fight in 1637. The latter arranged to have Mr. Digges abducted and impressed into military service![30] It stands to reason that such players probably presented discipline problems for the career military leaders. Undoubtedly this explains a newspaper notice of 1724, which read,

> We hear that the Musick belonging to the 2d Regiment of Guards have been this Week at Richmond to beg their Royal Highnesses Pardon for their ill Conduct on the Thames some Days ago at Richmond, when attending a certain Person of Distinction, and were generously forgiven.[31]

The trumpeters seem to have been paid more than most musicians, not only because of their constant use for giving signals but because they had to serve as ambassadors when the nobles traveled. The trumpeter was considered the equivalent of a passport, or a "white flag," and was supposed to be allowed to cross enemy lines unharmed. Dryden demon-

[26] Peter Panoff, *Militarmusik* (Berlin, 1944), 130.

[27] Farmer, *Military Music*, 48.

[28] Peter Panoff, *Militarmusik* (Berlin, 1944), 130.

[29] Farmer, *Handel's Kettledrums* (London, 1965), 43.

[30] Farmer, Ibid., 37.

[31] Edward Croft-Murray, "The Wind-Band in England," in *Music & Civilisation* (London, 1980), 142.

strates this tradition in his play, *King Arthur* (II, ii), when a trumpet behind one side of the stage signals for a parley and is answered by the opposing trumpet on the other side.[32] Another diary, of one who accompanied the Earl of Arundel on a journey through Germany in 1636, mentions,

> ... whilst our trumpeter was allowed to visit ... the castle in order to ask French permission for our further passage.[33]

Sad to say, this particular trumpeter was murdered when the party was near Nürnberg.[34]

> His Excellency's Gentleman of the Horse and his Trumpeter, together with the corpse of their guide, the Postmaster, were found ... It appeared that each must have witnessed the death agonies of his companions. The head of the Gentleman of the Horse had been shattered by a pistol shot, the Trumpeter's head had been cut off and the guide's head had been split open.[35]

[32] A similar exchange is found in *The Spanish Fryar* (V, i).

[33] Francis Springell, *Connoisseur & Diplomat* (London, 1936), 89.

[34] When another royal trumpeter was killed while on a diplomatic mission to Poland, the court documents seem more concerned with the loss of the king's silver trumpet. See Richard McGrady, "The Court Trumpeters of Charles I and Charles II," in *The Music Review* (1974), 227.

[35] Ibid., 80.

Part II

Jacobean Views on Music

10
Views by English Musicians of the Baroque

ONE FINDS, among these English musicians of the Baroque Period, virtually no discussion of aesthetics beyond the subject of music. An exception is an interesting discussion by Charles Avison on the analogies between music and painting. Avison assumes that most of his public will be familiar with the basic aesthetic principles of the latter, but not the former, therefore he writes of the analogies between painting and music as a means of explaining musical composition to the general reader.[1] Both arts, he finds, are based on geometry and a sense of proportion in their subject. Whereas painting depends on design, coloring and expression, music depends on melody, harmony and expression. As Avison considers melody the most important element of music, he describes the relationship of the other elements as follows:

> Melody, or air, is the work of invention, and therefore the foundation of the other two [harmony and expression], and directly analogous to design in painting. Harmony gives beauty and strength to the established melodies, in the same manner as coloring adds life to a just design. And, in both cases, expression arises from a combination of the other two, and is no more than a strong and proper application of them to the intended subject.

He considers the mixture of light and shade in painting to be analogous to consonance and dissonance in music. Likewise, the elements of fore-ground, the effect of distance,

[1] Charles Avison, *An Essay on Musical Expression* [London, 1753] (New York: Broude Reprint, 1967), 20ff. Avison (1709–1770) was an organist and composer.

etc., in painting corresponds in music to the ranges of the various parts, treble, tenor and bass. A charming analogy concerns the viewer and listener. Just as a viewer must stand at a certain distance to appreciate perspective in a painting, so the listener must be removed somewhat from the sound source to properly hear the correct balances.

> To stand close by a bassoon, or double-bass, when you hear a concert, is just as if you should plant your eye close to the fore-ground when you view a picture; or, as if in surveying a spacious edifice, you should place yourself at the foot of a pillar that supports it.

Regarding general definitions of music, we continue to find among the seventeenth century musicians strong traces of the views of the Scholastic teachings of the medieval universities. Charles Butler, writing in 1636, clearly reflects the old distinction between theoretical and practical music when he defines music as consisting of what he calls "Precepts and Uses or Ends."[2] Precepts are taught through singing and composition; the Ends are two: Ecclesiastical, for the service of God, and Civil, for the solace of men. Butler's discussion of musical instruments reflects the final period in which the consort principle is a dominant aesthetic principle and he mentions in particular the popularity of the "Set of Viols and Set of Waits," the latter being a reference to the civic wind bands.

[2] Charles Butler, *The Principles of Musik in Singing and Setting* [1636] (New York: Da Capo Press, 1970), 93. Butler (d. 1647) was a music theorist attached to Oxford whose interests extended to agriculture and grammar.

We see a specific remnant of Scholasticism in Christopher Simpson who, as late as 1667, still refers to music as a member of the family of mathematics.

> In this divine use and application, music may challenge a preeminence above all the other mathematical sciences as being immediately employed in the highest and noblest office that can be performed by men or angels.[3]

He then divides music into three categories, the first of which is the "theory or mathematical part." Next is the practical part, "which designs, contrives and disposes those sounds into so many strange and stupendous varieties." The third is the performer, after which he adds "any one of which

[3] Christopher Simpson, *A Compendium of Practical Music*, Second Edition of 1667 (Oxford: Blackwell, 1970), 76. Simpson (d. 1669) was a composer of string music, especially for the viola da gamba.

three parts of music considered in itself is a most excellent art or science."

Simpson follows this definition of music with a comment that vocal music is made "for the solace and civil delight of man." Among the vocal forms he first mentions the madrigal, followed by an interesting observation (for 1667!) on the influence of Italian opera, "Dramatic or Recitative Music is yet something of a stranger to us here in England."

He ranks the fantasia [*fancy*] as the highest kind of instrumental music, which he says unfortunately few people understand, "their ears being better acquainted and more delighted with light and airy music." Following this, "in dignity," is the pavan, which he notes was once ordained for grave and stately dancing, but now has "grown up to a height of composition made only to delight the ear."

By the second half of the seventeenth century, however, most definitions of music had left mathematics behind and had begun to focus on music's relationship to the emotions. John Playford, for example, writing in 1674, found,

> Music is an Art unsearchable, Divine and Excellent, by which a true concordance of sounds or harmony is produced, that rejoiceth and cheereth the hearts of men.[4]

[4] John Playford, *An Introduction to the Skill of Music* [1674] (Ridgewood: Gregg Press, 1966), preface. Playford (1623–1686) was a publisher and amateur composer and theorist.

An important new influence on aesthetics was the rise of public concerts, which made the element of popularity, or fashion, a topic of concern. Thomas Mace, from his rather serious religious perspective, was at a loss to understand how mere public taste could take precedence over principles of art.

> But I cannot understand, how Arts and Sciences should be subject unto any such Fantastical, giddy or inconsiderate toyish conceits, as ever to be said to be in Fashion, or out of Fashion.[5]

[5] Thomas Mace, *Musick's Monument* [1676] (Paris: Editions du Centre National de la Recherche Scientifique, 1966), 232ff. Mace (1613–1709) was a "clerk" at Trinity College, Cambridge.

In this regard he specifically objected to the current fashion of significantly doubling the upper voice in ensembles, thereby emphasizing melody over harmony and disrupting the equality of parts found in former styles.

By the end of the Baroque, we see in Avison a complete break with Scholastic dogma. It must have been much more dramatic at the time, than it seems to us, for him to state that musical communication is *not* of the realm of Reason.

> After all that has been, or can be said, the energy and grace of musical expression is of too delicate a nature to be fixed by words: it is a matter of taste, rather than of reasoning, and is, therefore, much better understood by example than by precept.[6]

[6] Avison, *An Essay on Musical Expression*, 81.

For some musicians, the contemplation of the nature of music led to an almost Platonic view of music as a representative of a larger, divine harmonic order of the universe. This seems to have been in mind, for example, when the composer and organist, Martin Peerson (1572–1650) wrote in the dedication for his *Mottets or Grave Chamber Music* (1630),

> ... that heaven upon earth, which it found here, in Musicke and Harmonicall proportions, the being whereof is beyond Mortalitie and regulates the whole frame of nature in her being and Motions.[7]

[7] Quoted in Peter Walls, "London, 1603–49," in *The Early Baroque Era* (Englewood Cliffs: Prentice Hall, 1994), 283.

Some Englishmen searched for more concrete connections between the mystery of music and the physical laws of Nature. One of these was Robert Flud (1574–1637), a philosopher and physician whose extensive writings were largely ignored in the generations following him because he was a known member of the Rosicrucians.[8] Flud imagined the Earth and planets organized in a cosmic musical instrument, which he called a Mundane Monochord. The following, taken from his book, *De Musica Mundana* (1617), will give the reader some indication of the nature of his speculation.

[8] Flud was educated in the arts at Oxford, but his interests turned to physics. He traveled widely before resuming his studies in chemistry and physics. He eventually took a degree in medicine and became a member of the college of physicians in London.

> But it is to be considered that in this mundane monochord the consonances, and likewise the proper intervals, measuring them, cannot be otherwise delineated than as we divide the instrumental monochord into proportional parts; for the frigidity, and also the matter itself, of the earth, as to the thickness and weight thereof, naturally bears the same proportion to the frigidity as the matter of the lowest region, in which there is only one fourth part of the natural light

and heat, as 4 to 3, which is the sesquitertia proportion; in which proportion a diatessaron consists, composed of three intervals, namely, water, air, and fire; for the earth in mundane music is the same thing as the fundamental in music, unity in arithmetic, or a point in geometry; it being as it were the term and sound from which the ratio of proportional matter is to be calculated. Water therefore occupies the place of one tone, and the air that of another interval more remote; and the sphere of fire, as it is only the summit of the region of the air, kindled or lighted up, possesses the place of a lesser semitone. But in as much as two portions of this matter are extended upwards as far as to the middle heaven to resist the action of the supernatural heat; and the same number of parts of light, act downwards against these two portions of matter, these make up the composition of the sphere of the sun, and naturally give it the attribute of equality, and by that means the sesquialtera proportion is produced, in which three parts of the lower spirit or matter of the middle heaven are opposed to the two parts of the solar sphere, producing the consonant diapente: for such is the difference between the moon and the sun, as there are four intervals between the convexity of this heaven and the middle of the solar sphere, namely, those of the entire spheres of the moon, Mercury, and Venus, compared to full tones, and the half part of the solar sphere, which we have compared to the semitone ...

Christopher Simpson was moved by what he regarded as apparent, if mysterious, relationships between music and the rest of creation.

I cannot but wonder, even to amazement, that from no more than three concords (with some intervening discords) there should arise such an infinite variety, as all the music that ever has been or ever shall be composed. And my wonder is increased by a consideration of the seven gradual sounds or tones, from whose various positions and intermixtures those concords and discords do arise. These gradual sounds are distinguished in the scale of music by the same seven letters which in the calendar distinguish the seven days of the week; to either of which, the adding of more is but a repetition of the former over again.

The mysterious number of seven, leads me into a contemplation of the universe, whose creation is delivered unto our capacity (not without some mystery) as begun and finished in seven days, which is thought to be figured long since by Orpheus his seven stringed lyre. Within the circumference of this great universe, be seven globes or spherical bodies in continual motion, producing still new and various figures, according to their diverse positions one to another. When with these I compare my seven gradual sounds, I cannot but admire the resemblance of their harmonies, the concords of the one so exactly answering to the aspects of the other; as an unison to conjunction, an octave to an opposition; the middle consonants to a diapason, to the middle aspects of an orb; as a third, fifth, sixth, in music, to a trine, quartile, sextile in the Zodiac. And as these by moving into such and such aspects bodies; so those, by passing into such and such concords, transmit into the ear an influence of sound, which doth not only strike the sense, but even affect the very soul, stirring it up to a devout contemplation of that divine principle from whence all harmony proceeds; and therefore very fitly applied to sing and sound forth his glory and praise.[9]

[9] Christopher Simpson, *Division-Violist* (1654), here (London: Curwen, 1965, facsimile of 1665 edition, 1965), 23ff.

On the Purposes of Music

FOLLOWING THE MOVEMENT begun by the humanists during the late Renaissance, English writers during the seventeenth century began to focus on the emotions as a fundamental component of aesthetics. It was in the context of this background of the earlier humanists, that Charles Butler (1636) spoke of emotions in terms of the "divine frenzy" mentioned by the ancient Greek philosophers.

> [Good composing is impossible] unless the Author, at the time of Composing, be transported as it were with some Musical fury; so that himself scarce knoweth what he doth, nor can presently give a reason for his doing.[10]

[10] Butler, *The Principles of Musik*, 92.

The most interesting commentary on this question, in a general sense, is by Charles Avison, who began his book on aesthetics in music with this sentence:

> If we view this art in its foundations, we shall find, that by the constitution of man it is of mighty efficacy in working both on his imagination and his passions.[11]

[11] Avison, *An Essay on Musical Expression*, 2ff.

While Avison recognized that music enters our awareness through the external senses, he found it was rather the internal senses which understand and profit.

> The capacity of receiving pleasure from these musical sounds, is, in fact, a peculiar and internal sense; but of a much more refined nature than the external senses: for in the pleasures arising from our internal sense of harmony, there is no prior uneasiness necessary, in order to our tasting them in their full perfection ... It is their peculiar and essential property, to divest the soul of every unquiet passion, to pour in upon the mind, a silent and serene joy, beyond the power of words to express, and to fix the heart in a rational, benevolent, and happy tranquility.

Avison gives great emphasis to his belief that music creates only "sociable and happy passions" and tends to subdue those which are contrary to this. He recognizes that it is generally believed that the power of music can affect every emotion, however,

> I would offer to the consideration of the public, whether this is not a general and fundamental error. I would appeal to any man, whether ever he found himself urged to acts of selfishness, cruelty, treachery, revenge, or malevolence by the power of musical sounds? Or if he ever found jealousy, suspicion, or ingratitude engendered in his breast, either from harmony or discord? I believe no instance of this nature can be alleged with truth. It must be owned, indeed, that the force of music may urge the passions to an excess, or it may fix them on false and improper objects, and may thus be pernicious in its effects: But still the passions which it raises, though they may be misled or excessive, are of the benevolent and social kind, and in their intent at least are disinterested and noble.

He immediately recognizes that some readers might consider the emotions of terror and grief to be an exception to what he has just written. But, no,

> terror raised by musical expression is always of that grateful kind, which arises from an impression of something terrible to the imagination, but which is immediately dissipated, by

> a subsequent conviction, that the danger is entirely imaginary ... As to grief, it will be sufficient to observe that as it always has something of the social kind for its foundation, so it is often attended with a kind of sensation, which may with truth be called pleasing.

He admits it is difficult to give a reason for his theory, but ventures the explanation that since music immediately places the mind in a pleasurable state, the mind tends to associate with those emotions most agreeable to it.

> From this view of things therefore it necessarily follows, that every species of musical sound must tend to dispel the malevolent passions, because they are *painful*; and nourish those which are benevolent, because they are *pleasing*.

From the perspective of the seventeenth century composer, the question of the emotions often began with the relationship with the words in sung poetry. For William Byrd, writing in his *Gradualia* (1605), the words were indeed the point of origin for his inspiration.

> There is a certain hidden power, as I learned by experience, in the thoughts underlying the words themselves; so that, as one meditates upon the sacred words and constantly and seriously considers them, the right notes, in some inexplicable manner, suggest themselves quite spontaneously.[12]

[12] Quoted in Robert Donnington, *The Interpretation of Early Music* (New York, 1964), 112.

John Playford, quoting, in 1647, an unnamed "English gentleman who had lived long in Italy," reflects the growing influence of Italian music in England and the subsequent idea that even improvisation should be tied to the emotions.

> To which manner I have framed my last Ayres for one voice to the Theorbo, not following that old way of composition, whose music not suffering the words to be understood by the hearers, for the multitude of divisions made upon short and long syllables, though by the vulgar such singers are cried up for famous. But I have endeavored in those my late compositions, to bring in a kind of music, by which men might as it were talk in harmony, using in that kind of singing a certain noble neglect of the song (as I have often heard at Florence by the actors in their singing operas) in which I

endeavored the imitation of the conceit of the words, seeking out the chords more or less passionate ... But, as I said before, those long windings and turnings of the voice are ill used, for I have observed that divisions have been invented, not because they are necessary unto a good fashion of singing, but rather for a certain tickling of the ears of those who do not well understand what it is to sing passionately; for if they did, undoubtedly divisions would have been abhorred, there being nothing more contrary to passion than they are ... Whereas those that well understand the conceit and the meaning of the words ... and can distinguish where the passion is more or less required. Which sort of people we should endeavor to please with all diligence, and more to esteem their praise, than the applause of the ignorant vulgar.[13]

[13] Playford, *An Introduction to the Skill of Music*, 38ff.

Similarly, in 1667 Christopher Simpson wrote,

When you compose music to words, your chief endeavor must be that your notes do aptly express the sense and affections [*humour*] of them. If they be grave and serious, let your music be such also; if light, pleasant or lively, your music likewise must be suitable to them. Any passion of love, sorrow, anguish and the like is aptly expressed by chromatic notes and bindings. Anger, courage, revenge, etc., require a more strenuous and stirring movement. Cruel, bitter, harsh, may be expressed with a discord which, nevertheless, must be brought off according to the rules of composition.[14]

[14] Simpson, *A Compendium of Practical Music*, 77.

The most important English writer on this subject was Charles Avison, who wrote with great insight. In beginning a chapter called "On Musical Expression, as it relates to the Composer," Avison first dismisses text-painting as a proper source of communicating feeling in music. He makes the very important point that such devices only cause the listener to focus on secondary effects and not on the genuine feelings.

Now all these I should choose to style imitation, rather than expression; because, it seems to me, that their tendency is rather to fix the hearers attention on the similitude between the sounds and the things which they describe, and thereby to excite a reflex act of the understanding, than to affect the heart and raise the passions of the soul.[15]

[15] Avison, *An Essay on Musical Expression*, 57ff.

Likewise, music composed for poetry can only assist the emotion of the words and cannot literally be synonymous with the words. In fact, he suggests, the composer who strives to "catch each particular epithet or metaphor" of the poetry will always, in the end, "hurt the true aim of his composition." His aim, according to Avison, must be rather to reflect the emotions in a more general sense.

> What then is the composer, who would aim at true musical expression, to perform? I answer, he is to blend such an happy mixture of melody [air] and harmony, as will affect us most strongly with the passions or affections which the poet intends to raise: and that, on this account, he is not principally to dwell on particular words in the way of imitation, but to comprehend the poet's general drift or intention ... If he attempts to raise the passions by imitation, it must be such a temperate and chastised imitation, as rather brings the object before the hearer, than such a one as induces him to form a comparison between the object and the sound. For, in this last case, [the listener's] attention will be turned entirely on the composer's art, which must effectually check the passion. The power of music is, in this respect, parallel to the power of eloquence: if it works at all, it must work in a secret and unsuspected manner.[16]

[16] Ibid., 69ff. In a footnote, Avison reflects that the "wonderful effects" attributed to the ancient Greek composers must have been to "the pure simplicity of melody."

Some modern clinical research indicates that musical perception in the brain depends greatly on a genetic repertoire of melodic patterns. It is most likely that these melodic patterns carry the basic emotional keys to which we, as listeners, respond. Therefore, as Avison correctly observes, a strophic song, which has a variety of verses to the same melody, is based on an impossible aesthetic premise. Avison calls this new style a "remarkably ridiculous" one of the English of his day.

> I mean our manner of setting a single trifling air, repeated to many verses, and all of them, perhaps, expressive of very different sentiments or affections, than which, a greater absurdity cannot possibly be imagined, in the construction of any musical composition whatsoever.[17]

[17] Ibid., 83ff.

In his search for melody, Avison cautions the composer to "shun all the means of catching the common air [meaning popular melodies], which so strangely infects and possesses too many composers." Better if he banish himself from "almost every place of public resort and fly, perhaps, to monasteries, where the genuine charms of harmony may often be found."[18]

[18] Ibid., 87.

Avison makes some interesting comments relative to the character of individual instruments and the expression of emotions. The oboe, he says, should be associated with gay and cheerful music and, interestingly enough, the transverse flute with "languishing or melancholy style."[19] The role of the trumpet is to animate and inspire courage, whereas the horn is to enliven and clear the spirits.

[19] Ibid., 112ff.

Some of Avison's most interesting and valuable comments deal with the nature of the familiar Italian words which today we associate primarily with tempo. It is the character of such words as "Allegro" or "Adagio," not the "time or measure," he says, which distinguished their particular expression and he ties this idea with what he calls the three "species of music: Church, Theater and Chamber." Therefore,

> the same terms which denote Lively and Gay, in the Opera, or Concert Style, may be understood in the practice of Church Music as Cheerful and Serene ... Wherefore, Allegro [in church music] should always be performed somewhat slower than is usual in concerti and opera.[20]

[20] Ibid., 123ff.

Turning to the perspective of the performer, we begin by quoting an anonymous Jacobean song which reminds us that the performer has no doubt always, to some degree, performed to please himself.

> My mistress is in musicke passinge skillful
>   and singes & plaies her part at the first sight
> But in her play she is exceeding wilfull
>   & will no plaie but for her owne delight.
> Nor touche a stringe nor plaie a pleasinge straine
>   unless you catch her in a merie vaine.[21]

[21] Quoted in Walls, "London, 1603–49," 286.

The most interesting comments relative to the performer at this time reflect the considerable freedom, by modern standards, permitted in expressing emotions. John Playford reflects an unusual degree of rubato.

> We see how necessary a certain judgment is for a musician, which sometimes useth to prevail above art
>
> ......
>
> I call that the noble manner of singing, which is used without tying a man's self to the ordinary measure of time, making many times the value of the notes less by half, and sometimes more according to the conceit of the words; whence proceeds that excellent kind of singing with a graceful neglect.[22]

[22] Playford, *An Introduction to the Skill of Music*, 46, 52. Today we use the word, "rubato," in place of "graceful neglect."

Mace, in making similar comments in 1676, seems to suggest that the freedom in time extended even to form. If, he says, the music falls into sections, these may be played,

> according as they best please your own fancy, some very briskly, and courageously, and some again gently, lovingly, tenderly and smoothly.
>
> ......
>
> Beginners must learn strict time; but when we come to be masters, so that we can command all manner of time, at our own pleasures; we then take liberty ... to break time; sometimes faster and sometimes slower, as we perceive, the nature of the thing requires.[23]

[23] Mace, *Musik's Monument*, 429, 432.

Avison's discussion of the role of the performer, with respect to the communication of emotions in music, takes a surprising turn. Avison had an unusually accurate perception of the importance of communicating emotion in music and he wrote at a time when the performer had much more freedom than the performer today. It appears surprising, therefore, to find him recommending adherence to the score. Actually, we must view his comment in the context of his concern that Baroque music had become a performer's art and his desire to restore the center of aesthetic attention on the composer. In any case, he must have been one of the first to argue for a performance aesthetic which would become so characteristic of our own time.

> For, as musical expression in the composer, is succeeding in the attempt to express some particular passion; so in the

performer, it is to do a composition justice, by playing it in a taste and style so exactly corresponding with the intention of the composer, as to preserve and illustrate *all* the beauties of his work.[24]

[24] Avison, *An Essay on Musical Expression*, 107ff.

Since, as Aristotle established, aesthetics in the performing arts only has real meaning in the observer, we find particularly interesting comments on the seventeenth century listener. First, there is William Byrd's plea for a contemplative listener, in the preface to his *Psalmes, Songs and Sonnets* of 1611.

> Only this I desire; that you will be but as careful to hear them well expressed, as I have been both in the composing and correcting of them. Otherwise the best song that ever was made will seem harsh and unpleasant, for that the well expressing of them, either by voices or instruments is the life of our labors, which is seldom or never well performed at the first singing or playing. Besides a song that is well and artificially made cannot be well perceived nor understood at the first hearing, but the oftener you shall hear it, the better cause of liking you will discover: and commonly that song is best esteemed with which our ears are most acquainted.[25]

[25] Quoted in Donnington, *The Interpretation of Early Music*, 117.

One vivid portrait of an attentive audience is found in a description of a performance of Handel.

> The audience was so enchanted with this performance, that a stranger who should have seen the manner in which they were affected, would have imagined they had all been distracted.[26]

[26] J. Mainwaring, *Memoirs of Handel* (1760), quoted in Donnington, Ibid., 96.

This suggestion of the distracted minds of the listeners was also mentioned by James Talbot, writing of the Sarabande in 1690. He describes it as soft and passionate in character, "apt to move the Passions and to disturb the tranquility of the Mind."[27]

[27] Quoted in Ibid., 402.

On "Ethos"

By Ethos, or the Doctrine of Affections, we go beyond merely communicating emotions to the listener to the idea that music can specifically affect the character of the listener. Charles

Butler, in 1636, expresses this idea in language similar to that used by nearly all early writers.

> Music ... having a great power over the affections of the mind, by its various Modes produces in the hearers various affects.[28]

[28] Butler, *The Principles of Musik*, 112.

John Playford, in 1674, is much more specific.

> Nor doth music [not] only delight the mind of man, and beast, and birds, but also conduceth much to bodily health by the exercise of the voice in song, which doth clear and strengthen the lungs, and if to be also joined the exercise the limbs, none need fear asthma or consumption; the lack of which exercise is often the death of many students: Also much benefit hath been found thereby, by such as have been troubled with defects in speech, as stammering and bad utterance. It gently breathes and vents the Mourners grief, and heightens the joy of them that are cheerful: it abates spleen and hatred, the valiant soldier in fight is animated when he hears the sound of the trumpet, the fife and drum: All mechanical artists do find it cheers them in their weary labors. Scaliger gives a reason of these effects, because the spirits about the heart taking in that trembling and dancing air into the body, are moved together, and stirred up with it; or that the mind, harmonically composed, is roused up at the tunes of music. And farther, we see even young babes are charmed asleep by their singing nurses, nay the poor laboring beasts at plow and cart are cheered by the sound of music, though it be but their master's whistle.[29]

[29] Playford, *An Introduction to the Skill of Music,* preface. Playford also relates,

> Myself, as I traveled some years since near Royston, met a herd of stags, about twenty, upon the road following a bagpipe and a violin, which while the music played they went forward, when it ceased they all stood still.

Thomas Mace made fervent testimonials to the power of music. He begins in a passage where he is lamenting the music of former times, specifically the consort music of the early seventeenth century.

> We had for our grave music, Fancies of 2, 3, 5, and 6 parts to the organ; interposed (now and then) with some pavans, allmaines, solemn, and sweet delightful ayres; all of which (as it were) so many Pathetical Stories, Rhetorical and sublime discourses; subtle, and acute argumentations, so suitable, and agreeing to the inward, secret, and intellectual faculties of the soul and mind; that so set them forth according to their true praise, there are no words sufficient in language; yet

what I can best speak of them, shall be only to say, that they
have been to myself (and many others), as divine raptures,
powerfully captivating all our unruly faculties, and affections
(for the time) and disposing us to Solidity, Gravity, and
Good Temper, making us capable of Heavenly, and Divine
influences.

It is a great pity few believe thus much; but far greater, that
so few know it.[30]

The fashion today, he laments, has replaced these things with an emphasis on the virtuoso performer, "the Great Idol," and music,

> which is rather fit to make a man's ears glow, and fill his
> brains full of frisks, etc., than to season, and sober his mind,
> or elevate his affection to Goodness.

During his discussion of country church music, Mace's heartfelt testimonial to the moral virtues of music becomes more personal.

> For if [children] be once truly principled in the grounds
> of piety and music when they are young, they will be like
> well-seasoned vessels, fit to receive all other good things to
> be put into them. And I am not only subject to believe, but
> am very confident, that the vast jarrings, the dischording-
> untunableness, over-spreading the face of the whole earth,
> might be much rectified, and put into tune sooner this way,
> than by any other way that can be thought upon.
>
> This I speak from an experience in my own soul, who am a
> man subject to the passions and imperfections of the worst of
> men. Yet by this virtue, this sublime elixir of musical and har-
> monical divinity, have found as much (in a comparative way)
> as this comes to, upon my own soul and violent passions.
>
> It cannot be too often repeated, how the evil spirit departed
> from Saul, when David played upon his harp. True music
> being a certain Divine-Magical-Spell, against all diabolical
> operations in the souls of men. But how little this is taken
> notice of, believed, or regarded by most, is grievous and
> lamentable to be thought upon.[31]

---

[30] Mace, *Musik's Monument*, 234. One of the interesting things Mace presents in his book is his design for the ideal performance hall.

[31] Ibid., 12.

11
Contemporary Views on Performance Practice

WHEN ORLANDO GIBBONS wrote in the preface to his *Madrigals and Mottets* of 1612,

> Experience tells us that songs of this nature are usually esteemed as they are well or ill performed,[1]

he was reflecting in part a transformation taking place during the seventeenth century in which the spotlight was moving from the composer toward the performer. Perhaps this also prompted John Playford's observation, "Art admitteth no Mediocrity."[2]

This attention to performance was extended to the smallest details, even to a single note, as Christopher Simpson observed, "Loud and soft sometimes occur in one and the same note." This is apparently what Roger North had in mind when he wrote,

> Learn to fill, and soften a sound, as shades in needlework, in sensation, so as to be like also a gust of wind, which begins from a soft air, and fills by degrees to a strength as makes all bend, and then softens away again into a temper, and so vanish.[3]

This concentration on the small detail by North is also a reflection of society's growing appreciation of music performance as an art. In another place he wrote,

[1] Quoted in Robert Donnington, *The Interpretation of Early Music* (New York, 1964), 117.

[2] John Playford, *An Introduction to the Skill of Music* [1674] (Ridgewood: Gregg Press, 1966), 41. Playford (1623–1686) was a publisher and amateur composer and theorist.

[3] Both quoted in Donnington, *The Interpretation of Early Music*, 487.

Music demands not only utmost spirit, and decorum in the composition, but little less than perfection in the performance, which is not always found.[4]

[4] Quoted in Ibid., 118.

A similar demand, here for better intonation, is found in one of the popular journals of the late Baroque, the *Tatler* for May 2, 1710:

> When I granted his request, I made one to him, which was, that the performers should put their instruments in tune before the audience came in; for that I thought the resentment of the Eastern Prince, who, according to the old story, mistook *tuning* for *playing*, to be very just and natural.

North also made some interesting specific recommendations regarding the quality of performance in ensemble playing. In his demand that the composer guide the rehearsal, he reminds us that before our century virtually every composition was composed for one performance. This is especially important to remember with regard to Baroque music, which was also usually written with the specific talents of the particular performers in mind.

> In solemn consorts, it would scarce be possible to proceed without some one director of the time; who is commonly the composer ...[5]

[5] Quoted in John Wilson, *Roger North on Music* (London: Novello, 1959), 105.

In another place, North makes an extraordinary recommendation regarding ensemble precision.

> To my very great hazard of reputation, I have affirmed that with 2 violins set to play the same part, if perfectly in tune to each other, it is better music is one goes a little before or behind the other, than when they play (as they zealously affect) together. For in that, nothing is achieved by the doubling, but a little loudness; but in the other way, by the frequent dissonances there is a pleasant seasoning obtained.[6]

[6] Ibid., 172.

This irregularity "gives an excellence few have observed or will allow" and "must be done with great moderation." In his view, however, it produces a,

> sparkle in the accord, as air and light doth to the eye in a landscape, and is an elegance which painters in their art

cannot describe ... for in all arts the sovereign beauty, as of women, are a *je ne scay quoy*.

The Baroque Period being one of significant improvement in the construction of all musical instruments, one might assume that some listeners were beginning to understand that the quality of the performance depended in part on the quality of the instrument. The great poet, John Milton, observed,

> I am luckier by far in my body of judges than either Orpheus or Amphion; for they merely applied their fingers cunningly and skillfully to little strings, attuned with pleasing harmony; and an equal portion of the charm of both lay in the strings themselves and in the proper and correct movement of the hands.[7]

And perhaps he had this partly in mind regarding the vocal instrument when he made an analogy based on a singer, "as a good song is spoiled by a lewd singer."[8] Certainly this was in the mind of the poet, Robert Herrick, when he wrote,

> Sing me to death; for till thy voice be clear,
> 'Twill never please the palate of my ear.[9]

With regard to the general topic of the quality of performance, one also finds comments on a variety of smaller detail. Francis Bacon (1561–1626), one of the great men of the age, for example, once commented on the quality of voice leading, cadences and vibrato.

> Is not the precept of a musician, to fall from a discord or harsh accord upon a concord or sweet accord, alike true in affection? Is not the improvisation [*trope*] of music, to avoid or slide from the close or cadence, common with the trope of rhetoric of deceiving expectation? Is not the delight of the quavering upon a stop in music the same with the playing of light upon the water?[10]

In another place he seemed sensitive to the placement of voices in the choir and their vocal quality.

> Dancing to song is a thing of great state and pleasure. I understand it, that the song be in choir, placed aloft, and

[7] "Oration," in *The Works of John Milton*, ed. Frank Patterson (New York: Columbia University Press, 1931-1938), XII, 211.

[8] "Animadversions," in Ibid., III, 176.

[9] *The Poetical Works of Robert Herrick* (Oxford: Clarendon Press, 1963), 152. Herrick (1591–1674) is considered one of the most gifted of the so-called Cavalier Poets. He was a graduate of Cambridge and became a prior in Devonshire.

[10] *The Advancement of Learning*, in *The Works of Francis Bacon* (Cambridge: Cambridge University Press, 1869), VI, 210.

accompanied with some broken [instrumental] music; and the verse be fitted to the device. Acting in song, especially in dialogues, has an extreme good grace; I say acting, not dancing (for that is a mean and vulgar thing); and the voices of the dialogue would be strong and manly (a bass and a tenor; no treble); and the verse high and tragical; not nice or dainty. Several choirs, placed one over against another, and taking the voice by catches, anthem-wise, give great pleasure.[11]

[11] "Of Masques and Triumphs," in Ibid., XII, 209ff.

Bacon wrote an essay, "Of Masques and Triumphs," in which he makes recommendations for the improvement of the masque, a basic entertainment form of Jacobean England and a form he had personally been involved with. Among the specific recommendations for the music of masques, it seems clear that for Bacon mere entertainment was not enough. He was clearly listening to the music.

> Let the songs be loud and cheerful, and not chirpings or pulings. Let the music likewise be sharp and loud, and well placed ...
> Let anti-masques not be long; they have been commonly of fools, satyrs, baboons, wild-men, antics, beasts, sprites, witches ... Let the music of them be recreative, and with some strange changes.

And this point is the inseparable "other side of the coin" of the quality of the performance, for the increased emphasis on the contemplative listener is a hallmark of the late Renaissance and Baroque Periods and a significant change from the long centuries of the Middle Ages when music was mostly functional and not an art. As the poet Robert Herrick pointed out, it was the listener who signifies the change in one from "flesh and blood" to an angel.

> So long as you did not sing, or touch your Lute,
> We knew it was flesh and blood, that there sat mute.
> But when your playing, and your voice came in,
> 'Twas no more you then, but a *Cherubin*.[12]

[12] *The Poetical Works of Robert Herrick*, 95.

Roger North also commented at length on the listener. In one place he makes it clear that contemplative listening was a new demand on the aristocratic audience. He points to an

Italian violinist, Nicolai Matteis, whose popularity in London was hampered by his artistic demands when he played at court, for he,

> behaved himself *fastously*; no person must whisper while he played, which sort of attention had not been the fashion at Court.[13]

[13] Wilson, *Roger North on Music*, 123.

Addison, in the *Spectator* for November 29, 1711, complains about the noise in the upper gallery of the opera and suggests that in the future a special conductor might be used to preside over the audience, "like the Director of a Consort, in order to awaken their attention, and beat time to their applauses."

As a listener, North was one of the earliest critics to notice the aesthetic effect resulting from the order of the compositions in a concert. Whether it be a fireworks display, or comedy or tragedy, he attributed the success with the audience with a plan in which the event began slowly and gradually increased in intensity. But in concerts he found only disorganized variety.

> A song, fugue, a solo or any single piece may be very good in their several kinds, but for lack of a due coherence of the whole, the company will not be pleased. And thus it is with the music exhibited in London publicly for a half crown. A combination of masters agree to make a consort as they call it, but do not submit to the government of any one, as should be done, to accomplish their design. And in the performance, each take his parts according as his opinion is of his own excellence. The master violin must have its solo, then joined with a lute, then a fugue, or sonata, then a song, then the trumpet and oboe, and so other variety, as it happens ... And the company know not whether all is ended, or anything is more to come, and what.[14]

[14] Ibid., 13ff.

An even worse idea for programming, in the view of North, was competition. While he admits the importance of aristocratic money in supporting music, he is much opposed to a current trend in London whereby nobles contribute money to a "pot" to be given to the performer who pleases them best in a concert. Competition in music, he says, has largely negative results.

> Instead of encouraging the endeavors of all, the happy victor only was pleased, and all the rest were discontented and some who thought they deserved better, were almost ready to [give up music] ... So much a mistake it is to force artists upon a competition, for all but one are sure to be malcontents.[15]

[15] Roger North, *Memoirs of Music*, ed. Edward Rimbault (London: Bell, 1846), 118ff. An advertisement in the London *Gazette* for March 21, 1699, reads,

> Several persons of quality having, for the encouragement of musick advanced 200 guineas, to be distributed in 4 prizes, the first of 100, the second of 50, the third of 30 and the four of 20 guineas shall be adjudged to compose the best ...

There is one aspect of music performance in which more depends on the listener than the performer. Through evolution, to make a *very* long story short, our brain has learned to "emphasize" higher pitches, beginning at about third space C in the treble clef. That is, we "hear" things louder than the actual fact; we hear something that cannot be confirmed on an oscilloscope. Common experience, therefore, has led conductors from at least the Renaissance to have the lower voices play louder in order to make the listener *imagine* a balance intended by the composer. This has also been commented on from time to time since the Renaissance and we find a typical comment in the Baroque by the great English theorist, Thomas Mace.

> You may add to your press a pair of violins, to be in readiness for any extraordinary jolly or jocund consort occasion; but never use them but with this proviso, viz., be sure you make an equal provision for them, by the addition and strength of basses, so that they may not out-cry the rest of the musick, the basses especially; to which end it will be requisite you store your press with a pair of lusty, full-sized Theorboes, always to strike in with your consorts or vocal musick, to which that instrument is most naturally proper.[16]

[16] Quoted in John Hawkins, *A General History of the Science and Practice of Music* (1776) (New York: Dover Reprint, 1963), II, 732.

A higher level of listener, of course, placed higher levels of expectation on the composer. A careful listener like Milton was now even noticing the quality of minor modulations, as we see in a passing reference he makes on the subject of smooth connections in writing,

> unless I can provide against offending the ear, as some Musicians are wont skillfully to fall out of one key into another without breach of harmony.[17]

[17] "An Apology Against a Pamphlet called A Modest Confutation of the Animadversion." (1642), in *The Works of John Milton*, III, 341.

In England one does not find as much discussion of singing as one finds in other countries. North's criticism of singing[18] is centered again on the quality of performance. As with instrumental music, his preference was for full, if not loud, sound.

[18] Quoted in Wilson, *Roger North on Music*, 215ff.

> They say the English have no good voices, because few sing well … The English have generally voices good enough, though not up to the pitch of warmer countries; witness the cries and ballad singers—some women singing in the streets with a loudness and drowns all other noise, and yet firm and steady. Now what a sound would that be in a theater, cultivated and practiced to harmony! … But come into the theater or music-meeting, and you shall have a woman sing like a mouse in a cheese, scarce to be heard, and for the most part her teeth shut.

Among North's objections to singers was that their training has been in the fundamentals of vocal training, but not in the essentials of ear-training and musicianship.

> They do not understand the art of music that sing in public, but are scholars and taught [by those] not able to do anything themselves, and consequently cannot well distinguish when they do well and when ill. For this reason they will be horribly out of tune; and all this by a little understanding would correct itself in others as also in themselves. If it be said, some have no ears and cannot; I answer, send them to shops and trades, and let not the public be molested with their lack of ears.

He also finds among singers, that "women are fearful of the distortion of the face, which is their *sanctum sanctorum*, and therefore the sound is checked."

Robert Herrick suggests in one of his poems that the voice is more appreciated if accompanied.

> Rare is the voice itself; but when we sing
> To the lute or viol, then 'tis ravishing.[19]

[19] *The Poetical Works of Robert Herrick*, 331.

North appreciated dynamic variation in performance, in particular a controlled crescendo and diminuendo. He thought the voice was most adapt at this, followed by wind instruments and then strings, including the new violin which he calls "the nightingale of instruments."[20] He thought it a

[20] Ibid., 218ff.

nice idea if phrases began loud and ended soft. Suspensions and dissonance should be "pressed hard," which creates attention in the listener.

> Then when you come off into a sweeter calmer air, as to a cadence, which often follows such passages, then be soft and easy, as much as to say, Be content all is well.

North, in his autobiography, allows the performer to add dynamic additions not indicated in the score.

> I was very much assisted as a performer by my knowledge of and acquaintance with the music. It gave me courage as well as skill to fill and swell where the harmony required an emphasis.[21]

He also observes that it might help performances if the soft passages were notated in red ink and the loud in black ink.

But one can go too far, as the poet, George Herbert, points out in a proverb,

> Great strokes make not sweet music.[22]

From our perspective, the most interesting problem in Baroque performance is improvisation. The Baroque lies midpoint between centuries beyond number when musicians performed before the invention of notation and our era when any musician who dares change the slightest thing on paper will be shot and his body never found.[23] It is this very problem that we see philosophers struggling with during the Baroque: How does one maintain a "live" quality in performance if one only reads from the page?

Charles Burney recalled Henry Purcell complaining that writing everything out robs music of its special quality of being performed in the present tense ["modernized by a judicious performer"]. When one plays written music, it is automatically music of the past ["obsolete and old fashioned"].

> Purcell, who composed for ignorant and clumsy performers was obliged to write down all the fashionable graces and embellishments of the times, on which accounts, his Music soon

[21] Quoted in Donnington, *The Interpretation of Early Music*, 489.

[22] "Jacula Prudentum," in *The Poems of George Herbert*, ed. Ernest Rhys (London: Walter Scott, 1885), 243. George Herbert (1593–1633) devoted most of his poetry to the Church of England, which he served as a rector near Salisbury. None of his poetry was published during his lifetime. Some publications refer to him as a "late orator of the University of Cambridge."

[23] We believe that one should not perform Baroque music unless one understands where improvisation is called for by the composer and is willing to do it.

became obsolete and old fashioned; whereas the plainness and simplicity of Corelli have given longevity to his works, which can always be modernized by a judicious performer, with very few changes or embellishments.[24]

Avison joins many others in observing that improvisation was "impossible to be expressed" in notation. His chief concern was that since every performer viewed this practice individually, the result was that the student became "discouraged in the progress of his study."[25]

Of course one can go too far with improvisation, as one English critic, Charles Butler, pointed out in 1636.

> Too much quaint Division, too much shaking and quavering of the Notes, all harsh straining of the Voices beyond their natural pitch, as they are odious and offensive to the ear; so do they drown the right sound of the words ... [26]

There also seemed to be a concern that ornamentation and improvisation must not sound academic. This point is charmingly made by Anthony Aston, who writes in 1748 of a boy whose singing was interrupted by a suggestion that he add improvisation [run a Division] in a certain place.

> O let him alone, said Mr. Purcell; he will grace it more naturally than you, or I, can teach him.[27]

North's interest in this subject centered primarily in the performance of ornaments. He begins by attempting to explain the contribution of ornamentation to the beauty of the composition.

> Gracing is like lace on a garment, which doth not give a beauty without an handsome contour of the whole. And such effect is there from the true, though the plainest, music; which may be wholly spoiled by the offering at graces, which loose the sound without giving any compensation for it, but is not much mended by even the best gracing, because the delicacy lies in true harmony of sound, which is the substance; the rest is pretty, but trifling, and of little weight ... But in common cadences, and passages, it is left to the performer ... [28]

......

[24] Charles Burney, *A General History of Music* [1776] (London, 1935), II, 443.

[25] Charles Avison, *An Essay on Musical Expression* [London, 1753] (New York: Broude Reprint, 1967), 126. Avison (1709–1770) was an organist and composer.

[26] Charles Butler, *Principles of Musik* (London, 1636), quoted in Donnington, *The Interpretation of Early Music*, 153.

[27] Anthony Aston, *Brief Supplement to Colley Cibber, Esq.* [1748], quoted in Donnington, *The Interpretation of Early Music*, 155.

[28] Quoted in Wilson, *Roger North on Music*, 27.

And a plain sound not thus set off, is like a dull plain color, or as a bad copy of a good picture, that wants the spirit and life, which a sparkling touch gives it. Thus a life and warmth in the coloring of a picture is well resembled to graces in music, that are not the body but the soul that enlivens it, or as the animal spirits that cannot be seen or felt, but yet make that grand difference between a living and a dead corpse.[29]

[29] Ibid., 28.

North is one of many musicians during the Baroque who, influenced by the long tradition of improvisation in music, questioned whether it is even possible to write on paper "all" of the music. In a discussion of "The Art of Gracing,"[30] North finds,

[30] Ibid., 149ff.

It is the hardest task that can be, to pen the manner of artificial Gracing of an upper part. It hath been attempted, and in print, but with woeful effect. One that hears, with a direct intent to learn, may be shown the way by a notation, but no man ever taught himself that way. The spirit of that art is incommunicable by writing, therefore it is almost inexcusable to attempt it.

He observes the growing tendency for composers to attempt to write everything out and reflects the objections by the performers to this new practice. His final comment here is very interesting. One often finds quoted an early critic who maintained that Italian composers of this period wrote what they wanted played and therefore there should be no further improvisation. We believe North's understanding is probably the more accurate, at least for music before the very end of the Baroque.

But to set them down in the music book is such pains, and for the continual use and smallness of them, so intricate, puzzling and unintelligible, that with the best musicians they are altogether omitted. But of late some masters, to encourage their scholars by ease, have in their printed songs done it. But if it be for the ease of scholars who have been taught, in remembering their lesson, it is very disadvantageous to the better performers ... for it is not easy to know which is the true note, and where the emphasis falls, so the beauty is lost. The Italians who I think may be our masters, never express [improvisation], but write the true note which governs the harmony, and leave the [improvisation] to the skill and capacity of the performer.

And again,

The most skillful of the elder Italians leave all those matters [ornamentation] to the performers, and write their music plain ... But they had the soul of music in their compositions, which the moderns, with their many motive and slurring ornaments, have corrupted.[31]

[31] Ibid., 263.

But, for the *Spectator* for October 25, 1711, the blame fell specifically on Italian opera for influencing musical taste to the extent that one now even heard improper improvisation in church. It tells a story about a visiting woman from the city who improvises during village church music:

But what gives us the most offense is her theatrical manner of singing the psalms. She introduces above fifty Italian Airs into the Hunderdth Psalm, and whilst we begin "All People" in the old solemn tune of our fore-fathers, she in quite a different key runs divisions on the vowels, and adorns them with the graces of Nicolini ... we are certain to hear her quavering them half a minute after us to some sprightly airs of the opera.

I am very far from being an enemy to church musick; but fear this abuse of it may make my parish ridiculous, who already look on the singing psalms as an entertainment, and not part of their devotion.

We conclude this brief survey of English commentary on improvisation by quoting from a pastoral poem of seventeenth century England by Richard Crashaw called "Musicks Duell."[32] Here we find a contest in music, a familiar element in the pastoral poems of the lyric poets of ancient Greece and Rome. The present poem includes an unusually vivid description of the technique of the lute player and it is for this reason that we quote it. The careful reader, with perhaps a little imagination to picture what the poet is describing, may find some rare clues here on what some seventeenth century improvisation actually sounded like.

[32] "Musicks Duell," in *The Complete Poetry of Richard Crashaw*, ed. George Williams (New York: New York University Press, 1972), 535ff.

The poem begins as the lute player is playing only to soothe himself.

> Under production of an Oak; there sat
> A sweet Lute-master: in whose gentle airs
> He lost the day's heat, and his own hot cares.

A nightingale flies to a nearby tree and sings in such a way that the lute player decides to challenge the bird to a musical duel. He,

> Awakes his Lute, and against the fight to come
> Informs it, in a sweet *Praeludium*
> Of closer strains, and ere the war begin,
> He lightly skirmishes on every string
> Charged with a flying touch ...

The bird counters with "a thousand sweet distinguished tones and reckons up in soft divisions." Then the player of the lute resumes:

> His nimble hands instinct then taught each string
> A capering cheerfulness; and made them sing
> To their own dance; now negligently rash
> He throws his arm, and with a long drawn dash
> Blends all together; then distinctly trips
> From this to that; then quick returning skips
> And snatches this again, and pauses there.

The bird begins again, "meets art with art" and "with tender accents" amazes the lute player. Now the lute player tries harder.

> Strains higher yet; that tickled with rare art
> The tattling strings (each breathing in his part)
> Most kindly do fall out; the grumbling bass
> In surly groans disdains the treble's grace.
> The high perched treble chirps at this, and chides,
> Until his finger (Moderator) hides
> And closes the sweet quarrel, rouses all
> Hoarce, shrill, at once; as when the trumpets call
> Hot Mars to the Harvest of Death's field, and woo
> Mens' hearts into their hands ...

When the bird sings again, our poet makes a reference to the importance of melody, one of the significant departures of the Baroque from the earlier polyphonic era.

... the sugared nest
Of her delicious soul, that there does lie
Bathing in streams of liquid melody;
Music's best seed-plot ...

Now the lute player plays for the last time.

Every smooth turn, every delicious stroke
Gives life to some new grace; thus doth he invoke
Sweetness by all her names; thus, bravely thus
(Fraught with a fury so harmonious)
The lute's light *Genius* now does proudly rise,
Heav'd on the surges of swollen Rhapsodies.
Whose flourish (Meteor-like) doth curl the air
With flash of high-born fancies: here and there
Dancing in lofty measures, and anon
Creeps on the soft touch of a tender tone:
Whose trembling murmurs melting in wild aires
Runs to and fro, complaining his sweet cares
Because those precious mysteries that dwell,
In musick's ravished soul he dare not tell,
But whisper to the world: thus do they vary
Each string his note, as if they meant to carry
Their Masters blest soul (snatcht out at his ears
By a strong ecstasy) through all the spheres
Of Musicks heaven; and seat it there on high
In the *Empyraeum* of pure Harmony.
At length (after so long, so loud a strife
Of all the strings, still breathing the best life
Of blest variety attending on
His fingers fairest revolution
In many a sweet rise, many as sweet a fall)
A full-mouthed *Diapason* swallows all.

Exhausted and unable to take another turn, the bird dies.

12
Jacobean Philosophers on Music

THE FIRST HALF of the seventeenth century in England, with its civil wars and the agitation by the Puritans, offered a poor climate for normal intellectual activities such as philosophy, prose or music. Indeed the reader will find in the following material a distinctly dark mood throughout. In addition there is that curious mixture of some remarkable objective thought juxtaposed with Puritan dogma. These Protestant preachers were capable of twisting any passage of scripture, or any reference from ancient literature, in order to amplify their severe demands of religious discipline. A typical example of the latter is John Bunyan's extension of the famous Greek temple inscription, to read, "Know thyself, what a vile, horrible, abominable sinner thou art."[1]

Throughout the Middle Ages the Church philosophers raged against emotion as the enemy of Reason. This resulted in a distinctly negative climate for music, of course, as music is fundamentally nothing more than a language of emotion. Now in seventeenth century England the new Puritan faith returns to the battle between Reason and the emotions. Joseph Hall, like nearly all clerics before him, warns that the emotions can overwhelm Reason. The emotions he calls the "secret factors of sin and Satan," which must be controlled by Reason and religion.

> If there be any exercise of Christian wisdom, it is in the managing of these unruly affections ... Reason has always

[1] "The Saints' Knowledge of Christ's Love," in *The Works of John Bunyan*, ed. George Offor (London: Blackie and Son, 1853), II, 28. John Bunyan (1628–1688) is considered the greatest prose writer among the Puritans of the seventeenth century. Only the Bible was so widely read in English homes for the subsequent three centuries. Bunyan was also the epitome of the "hell and brimstone" preacher.

been busy in undertaking this so necessary a moderation; wherein, although she has prevailed with some of colder temper; yet those which have been of more stubborn metal, like unto grown scholars, which scorn the ferule and ruled their minority, have still despised her weak endeavors ... Christianity gives not rules, but power, to avoid this short madness.[2]

[2] "Heaven upon earth," in *The Works of Joseph Hall, D.D.,* ed. Philip Wynter (New York: AMS Press, 1969), VII, 14ff. Joseph Hall (1574–1656) was a bishop in the Church of England.

Burton also acknowledges the great power, and danger, of the emotions in their capability to overwhelm Reason.

Good discipline, education, philosophy, divinity, may mitigate and restrain these passions in some few men at some times, but for the most part they domineer, and are so violent, that as a torrent, bears down all before, and overflows his banks, lays bare the fields, lays waste the crops, they overwhelm reason, judgment & pervert the temperature of the body. The charioteer is run away with, nor does the chariot obey the reins.[3]

[3] Robert Burton, *The Anatomy of Melancholy,* ed. Floyd Dell (New York: Tudor Publishing Company, 1938), 218. Robert Burton (1577–1640) was educated at Oxford and became vicar of St. Thomas Church in that town. Although this book has little validity in view of modern knowledge, it had a long history of influence, including Charles Lamb, Milton, Keats and Thackeray.

The physiological process by which the emotions overcome Reason, according to Burton, begins as follows:

Thus in brief, to our imagination comes, by the outward sense or memory, some object to be known (residing in the foremost part of the brain) which he, misconceiving or amplifying, presently communicates to the heart, the seat of all affections. The pure spirits forthwith flock from the brain to the heart by certain secret channels, and signify what good or bad object was presented; which immediately bends itself to prosecute or avoid it, and, withal, draws with it other humors to help it. So in pleasure, concur great store of purer spirits; in sadness, much melancholy blood; in ire, choler.[4]

[4] Ibid., 219.

Regarding the emotions in general, the Rev. Joseph Hall concludes the heart of man is wholly designed for fraud,

the affections mocking us in the object, measure, manner; and in all of them the heart of man is deceitful.[5]

[5] "The Great Impostor," in *The Works of Joseph Hall,* V, 163.

In discussing his contention that there is no difference between the emotion of anger and madness, he offers a rather extraordinary portrait of anger.

Raging madness is a short madness; what else argues the shaking of the hands and lips; paleness or redness or swelling of the face; glaring of the eyes; stammering of the tongue; stamping with the feet; unsteady motions of the whole body; rash actions ... distracted and wild speeches? And madness is nothing but continued rage.[6]

[6] "Holy Observations," in Ibid., VII, 541.

Later in this treatise he concludes "he is a rare man that has not some kind of madness reigning in him." The kinds of madness he had in mind were melancholy, pride, false devotion, ambition or covetousness, anger, laughing madness of extreme mirth, drunken madness, outrageous lust, curiosity and profaneness and atheism.[7]

[7] Ibid., 542.

For most English writers at this time, discussion on the emotions centered on melancholy. Harvey, in 1616, appeared interested in melancholy, but offered little discussion. He mentions that "physicians differ regarding the melancholy juice" and suggests melancholics lack pleasant disposition and talent and wonders if its origin were related to the "splen-stone."[8]

[8] William Harvey, *Lectures on the Whole of Anatomy*, trans. C. D. O'Malley (Berkeley: University of California Press, 1961), 93ff. William Harvey was physician to the king and a professor of the College of Physicians in London.

Burton associates a transitory form of melancholy with mortality itself, for every man experiences it on some occasion. This form comes and goes with,

> every small occasion of sorrow, need, sickness, trouble, fear, grief, passion, or perturbation of the mind, any manner of care, discontent, or thought, which causes anguish, dullness, heaviness and vexation of spirit, any ways opposite to pleasure, mirth, joy, delight, causing forwardness in us, or a dislike. In which equivocal and improper sense, we call him melancholy, that is dull, sad, sour, lumpish, ill-disposed, solitary, any way moved, or displeased. And from these melancholy dispositions no man living is free, no Stoic, none so wise, none so happy, none so patient, so generous, so Godly, so divine, that can vindicate himself; so well-composed, but more or less, some time or other he feels the smart of it. Melancholy in this sense is the character of Mortality.[9]

[9] Burton, *The Anatomy of Melancholy*, 125.

Finally, John Donne makes a rare association between color and the emotions.

> For we, when we are melancholy, wear black; when lusty, green; when forsaken, tawny; pleasing our own inward affections ...[10]

[10] John Donne, "Paradoxes and Problems," in *Selected Prose*, ed. Helen Gardner (Oxford: Clarendon Press, 1967), 12. John Donne (1573–1631) studied at both Oxford and Cambridge, but as a born Catholic was not permitted to receive a degree. After various attempts at professions brought him to poverty, he converted to the official Church, became famous for his sermons and eventually became Dean of St. Paul's.

We hope this brief background will prepare the reader for a similar, generally dark discussion of music.

Bunyan, in his *Pilgrim's Progress*, includes a passage with several metaphors based on music. We find most interesting here the characterization of the music of the trombone consort as "doleful," a description found in other literature of the sixteenth and seventeenth centuries in England, and the entire discussion of the bass part. Here Bunyan speaks through the character, Great-heart.

> The wise God will have it so; some must pipe, and some must weep. Now Mr. Fearing was one that played upon his bass; he and his fellows sound the sackbut, whose notes are more doleful than the notes of other music are; though, indeed, some say the bass is the ground of music. And, for my part, I care not at all for that profession that begins not in heaviness of mind. The first string that the musician usually touches is the bass, when he intends to put all in tune. God also plays upon this string first, when he sets the soul in tune for himself. Only here was the imperfection of Mr. Fearing, he could play upon no other music but this, till towards his latter end.
>
> I make bold to talk thus metaphorically, for the ripening of the wits of young readers; and because, in the book of Revelations, the saved are compared to a company of musicians that play upon their trumpets and harps, and sing their songs before the throne.[11]

In another figure of speech, Bunyan describes the cry of the beggar as a "shrill trumpet."[12]

[11] "Pilgrim's Progress," in *The Works of John Bunyan*, III, 215. For the "pipe" reference, see Matthew 11:16. For the Revelations passages, see 8:2 and 14:2.
[12] "Upon the Beggar," in *A Book for Boys and Girls*, in Ibid., III, 758.

On the Purpose of Music

The Puritan preacher, Joseph Hall, recognizes pleasure to be a purpose of music, but that does not mean he condones it for that purpose. He mentions the "lyre and harp, timbrel and flute" played at banquets referred to in Isaiah 5:12, but he can see only "profane and careless souls who spend their time in jollity and pleasure!"[13]

[13] "The Breathings of the Devout Soul," in *The Works of Joseph Hall*, VIII, 8ff.

> I am sure I have a thousand times more cause of joy and cheerfulness than the merriest of all those wild and jovial spirits: they have a world to play withal; but I have a God to rejoice in: their sports are trivial and momentary; my joy is serious and everlasting ...

The most familiar purpose for music given in early literature is to soothe either the performer or the listener. In one of his sermons, John Donne explains that God gave man music to settle his emotions.

> And, to tune us, to compose and give us a harmonie and concord of affections, in all perturbations and passions, and discords in the passages of this life ...[14]

[14] John Donne, "A Sermon preached at Pauls Crosse," in *Five Sermons* (Menston: Scolar Press, 1970), 3.

The Reverend Joseph Hall writes in several places of the special solace on hearing music at night.

> How sweetly doth this music sound in this dead season! In the daytime it would not, it could not so much affect the ear. All harmonious sounds are advanced by a silent darkness.

Hall finds a parallel in the glad tidings of salvation in the "night of persecution of our private affliction."[15] He expands on this idea in another work called "Songs in the Night."

[15] "Occasional Meditations," in *The Works of Joseph Hall*, X, 142.

> There is no time wherein [songs of praise] can be unseasonable: yea, rather, as all our artificial melody is wont to sound sweetest in the dark, so those songs are most pleasing to thee which we sing in the saddest night of our affliction ...
>
> The night is a dismal season, attended with solitude and horror, and an aggravation of those pains and cares whereof the day is in any sort guilty ... Songs in the night, are not, cannot be of nature's making, but are the sole gift of the heavenly Comforter.
>
> And if we, out of the strength of our moral powers, shall be setting songs to ourselves in the night of our utmost disconsolation, woe is me, how miserably out of tune they are! how harsh, how misaccented, how discordous even to the sense of our own souls, much more in the ears of the Almighty, in whom dwells nothing beneath an infinite perfection!
>
> But the songs that thou, O God, puttest into the mouths of thy servants in the night of their tribulation are so exquisitely harmonious, as that thine angels rejoice to hear them, and disdain not to match them with their hallelujahs in heaven.[16]

[16] "Souls in the Night," in Ibid., VII, 326.

In still another treatise, Hall recommends for those who "howl in the night of their affliction," singing at night.[17] He mentions here again his contention that music sounds best in the night.

Gervase Markham, in his *Countrey Contentments* (1615), places this purpose on almost a functional level.

> A gentleman should not be unskillful in Music, that whensoever either melancholy, heaviness of his thoughts, or the perturbations of his own fancies, stirreth up sadness in him, he may remove the same with some godly Hymn or Anthem, of which David gives him ample examples.[18]

The purpose of music to soothe, stated in this way, seems almost music therapy. But there are also in this literature some remarkable illustrations of actual music therapy. Burton, in his study of melancholy, lists what he considers the basic "diseases of the mind." Among "Dotage, Phrenzy, Madness, Hydrophobia, and Llycanthropia," we are surprised to find "St. Vitus' Dance." His discussion of this condition is rather interesting.

> S. Vitus' Dance; the lascivious dance, Paracelsus calls it, because they that are taken with it, can do nothing but dance till they be dead, or cured. It is so called, for that the parties so troubled were wont to go to S. Vitus for help, & after they had danced there a while, they were certainly freed. It is strange to hear how long they will dance, & in what manner, over stools, forms, tables; even great-bellied women sometimes (and yet never hurt their children) will dance so long that they can stir neither hand nor foot, but seem to be quite dead. Only in red clothes they cannot abide. Musick above all things they love, & therefore Magistrates in Germany will hire Musicians to play to them, and some lusty sturdy companions to dance with them. This disease hath been very common in Germany, as appears by those relations of Sckenkius, and Paracelsus in his book of Madness, who brags how many several persons he hath cured of it. Felix Platerus reports of a woman in Basle whom he saw, that danced a whole month together.[19]

In his discussion of the remedies for melancholy, Burton devotes a brief chapter to music. There have been many

[17] "The Breathings of the Devout Soul," in Ibid., VIII, 18ff.

[18] Quoted in Robert Donnington, *The Interpretation of Early Music* (New York, 1964), 117.

[19] Burton, *The Anatomy of Melancholy*, 124.

means by which philosophers and physicians have attempted to "exhilarate a sorrowful heart," he notes, but for him there is nothing so powerful as "a cup of strong drink, mirth, musick, and merry company."[20] After citing some high recommendations of music by ancient writers, Burton observes,

[20] Ibid., 478ff.

> Musick is a tonic to the saddened soul, a [powerful cannon] against melancholy, to rear and revive the languishing soul, affecting not only the ears, but the very arteries, the vital and animal spirits; it erects the mind, and makes it nimble. This it will effect in the most dull, severe, and sorrowful souls, expel grief with mirth, and if there be any clouds, dust, or dregs of cares yet lurking in our thoughts, most powerfully it wipes them all away, and that which is more, it will perform all this in an instant: cheer up the countenance, expel austerity, bring in hilarity, inform our manners, mitigate anger ... Our divine Musick, not only to expel the greatest griefs, but it doth extenuate fears and furies, appeases cruelty, abates heaviness, and to such as are watchful it causes quiet rest; it takes away spleen and hatred, be it instrumental, vocal, with strings, or wind; it leads us by the spirit, it cures all irksomeness and heaviness of the soul. Laboring men, that sing to their work, can tell as much, and so can soldiers when they go to fight, whom terror of death cannot so much affright, as the sound of trumpet, drum, fife, and such like musick, animates; the fear of death, as Censorinus informs us, musick drives away. It makes a child quiet, the nurse's song; and many times the sound of a trumpet on a sudden, bells ringing, a carman's whistle, a boy singing some ballad tune early in the street, alters, revives, recreates, a restless patient that cannot sleep in the night. In a word, it is so powerful a thing that it ravishes the soul, the Queen of the senses, by sweet pleasure (which is a happy cure) and corporal tunes, pacifies our incorporeal soul, and rules it without words, and carries it beyond itself, helps, elevates, extends it.

Burton continues with a number of illustrations and testimonials to the effectiveness of music therapy taken from early literature. In the last of these he quotes Scaliger, who, being always pleased with music and musicians, makes the interesting comment, "I am well pleased to be idle amongst them." Burton then concludes by commenting on some possible dangers of music.

> And what young man is not [pleased with music]? As it is acceptable and conducing to most, so especially to a melancholy man; provided always, his disease proceed not originally from it, that he be not some light Inamorato, some idle phantastick, who capers in conceit all the day long, and thinks of nothing else but how to make Jigs, Sonnets, Madrigals, in commendation of his mistress. In such cases Musick is most pernicious, as a spur to a free horse will make him run himself blind, or break his wind; for Musick enchants, as Menander holds, it will make such melancholy persons mad, and the sound of those Jigs and Horn-pipes will not be removed out of the ears a week after ... Many men are melancholy by hearing Musick, but it is a pleasing melancholy that it causes, and therefore to such as are discontent, in woe, fear, sorrow, or dejected, it is a most present remedy; it expels cares, alters their grieved minds, and eases in an instant.

Another ancient purpose of music is to play a role in courtship. John Donne recognizes music as one of three necessary tools for the conquest of women.

> They have found where was the easiest, and most accessible way, to solicit the chastity of a woman, whether *Discourse*, *Musicke*, or *Presents* ...[21]

On the other hand, Burton suggests that,

> To hear a fair young gentlewoman play upon the virginals, lute, viol, and sing to it ... are the chief delight of lovers.[22]

Finally, John Donne gives one purpose of music as being a rather functional tool for memory. Much of the instructions in the bible were given in the form of music, he maintains, for God then "was sure they would remember."[23]

There is very little discussion of performance techniques by these philosophers, but one comment on the prevalence of improvisation is very enlightening indeed. John Donne, in a letter of c. 1600, is speaking of the importance of not depending on books for one's education, but on personal observation and experience. Then, in analogy, he adds his observation that everyone would rather hear improvised music than that which was notated.

[21] John Donne, "A Sermon Preached at Saint Pauls upon Christmasse day. 1621," in *Selected Prose*, 209.

[22] Burton, *The Anatomy of Melancholy*, 699.

[23] John Donne, "A Lent Sermon Preached at White-hall, February 12, 1619," in *Selected Prose*, 183.

For both listeners and players are more delighted with voluntary than with sett musicke.[24]

There is little discussion among these philosophers of real art music, although John Bunyan includes two such scenes in his *Pilgrim's Progress*. First there are the "excellent virginals" in the dining room of Prudence, which she played before singing an "excellent" song about Jacob's ladder.[25] Later Christiana plays the viol, and her daughter, Mercy, the lute for their guests. Although the music is described as "merry disposed," it had no effect on Mr. Despondency.[26]

In these essays we have emphasized the importance of the contemplative listener as part of the definition of art music. We find it interesting, therefore, that Bunyan includes a poem, "Upon a Skillful Player on an Instrument," in his *A Book for Boys and Girls*, which goes further in its emphasis of the importance of the *educated* listener as a link in the communication of music.

> He that can play well on an instrument,
> Will take the ear, and captivate the mind
> With mirth or sadness; for that it is bent
> Thereto, as music in it place doth find.
> But if one hears that has therein no skill,
> (As often music lights of such a chance)
> Of its brave notes they soon be weary will:
> And there are some can neither sing nor dance.[27]

[24] John Donne, Letter [c. 1600], quoted in Ibid., 109. In a Sermon [Ibid., 278] Donne again criticizes the fact that education has limited us to seeing Nature through Aristotle's spectacles, medicine through Galen's and the universe through Ptolemy's.

[25] "Pilgrim's Progress," in *The Works of John Bunyan*, III, 204.

[26] Ibid., III, 229.

[27] "Upon a Skillful Player on an Instrument," in *A Book for Boys and Girls*, in *The Works of John Bunyan*, III, 761.

13
North on Music

ROGER NORTH (1653–1734), an amateur musician born to a well-to-do family and educated in law, brought to his writing a breadth of knowledge not enjoyed by his contemporaries who wrote on music and who were primarily working musicians. Of all the English Baroque writers on music before Avison, North is the only one who might also be called a philosopher.

Roger North seemed to understand through deduction and observation that the mind of man is clearly divided into rational and experiential forms of understanding, or what we refer to today as the left and right hemispheres of the brain. In the following passage he attempts to explain the distinction between rational learning, such as language, and music. After so many centuries during which higher education in music emphasized so-called "speculative," or as we would say today, theoretical, music, it is of the utmost significance that North attempts here to separate real musical learning from conceptual studies. In the final sentence he hints at the lesson we still have not learned, that conceptual teaching is foreign to what children instinctively love in music.

> The teaching of music and languages are very different, although the masters of the former affect the methods used by them of the other; that is, a sort of grammar to be [learned] by heart, whether it be or be not understood. The difference

lies in this, that languages are mere memory, and come from the arbitrary use of nations, and may be as well one way or another; and this use grammarians endeavor to reduce to rule, which must be learnt and remembered. But music is taken from nature itself, and depends on body in a physical sense, even as the mathematical sciences do, and takes place finally in our imagination and fancy; and therefore should be taught by explaining it to the understanding as well as by giving the rules to which the practice of it is reduced. And for this reason it is that in the musical science the rules are very few, and those but introductory as it were to show what the subject matter is, that the learner might not have the trouble of being an original inventor of the whole science ... And yet the real knowledge that belongs to music is dilated enough, and it is through that, that a man must learn the skill of a musician, whether he be showed it, or gathers it of himself by observation, as generally is done ... As for children, I think easier ways might be found than the soured and mysterious Gamut, which they must rehearse *antrorsum & retrorsum*, without the least proffer to them of an explanation of it.[1]

[1] Quoted in John Wilson, *Roger North on Music* (London: Novello, 1959), 59.

He touches on the distinction between language and music again in his attempt to explain what makes a good melody [*Ayre*], admitting he cannot express this in words.

The design here is not to frame rules for composition, which is of another nature, and must extend much wider to comprehend the many items of that art in which learners will need to be informed; but only to frame some Idea or Notion of [melody], which cannot fully be expressed in words.[2]

[2] Ibid., 84.

North is the first English writer of the Baroque to attempt to speculate on the nature of the perception of music. Like Aristotle he has observed that people tend to like best the music they already know. But this suggests that mere familiarity, and not intrinsic value, makes music so powerful in its communication. North seems to know this cannot be correct, but he is unable to explain it. It is interesting that we find here the earliest written rational for the *ritornello* principle.

I am of opinion that use goes a great way in the acceptance of music, and that be it really in true judgment better, if folks are not used to the manner they will not like it ... as if music had not the virtue intrinsically to please, but doth it by accident or custom, after some acquaintance with it. It is certain that the melody of music is improved by repetition, and is always better the second time than the first, and so on, till some novelty suppresseth it. For this reason it is that we have so many repeats and *ritornellos*.[3]

[3] Ibid., 69.

In another place he adds an additional explanation for the *ritornello* principle, which also reflects the ancient philosophers' concern for the transitory nature of music.

And the reason is, the sense is always better satisfied in a foreknowledge of what is to come, than to be surprised with anything entirely new, which comes, and is gone before it is enough reflected upon.[4]

[4] Ibid., 177ff.

North is also the first English musician to address the important aesthetic principle of universality in music. It is also a very important point that North makes here, that the aesthetic judgment rests with the listener. There is no other meaningful way to make sense of aesthetics in music.

I am of opinion that if a musical entertainment doth not please all tastes, it is not as it should be, and there is fault in the design, composition, or performance ... It seems better, and much more heroic, to calculate music by the measures of universal knowledge, and experience of Humane Nature, with all the passions and affections indifferently incident to all men; and this, done by a lofty instructed genius, and rightly understood, will assuredly pass for good [melody].[5]

[5] Ibid., 70ff.

North had obviously given much thought to the element of time in music and concluded that there is also something universal about the perception of time, perhaps even something genetic in character ("planted ... in our vital faculties").

As for the arm in swinging, I shall appeal to it as governed by pendulum law. Nothing unequal timed is pleasing, as if equality had planted its capital residence in our vital faculties.[6]

[6] Ibid., 95.

......

> Nothing of failure is less excused than missing time; for the audience being once possessed of a current measure, esteems it an injury to be interrupted by any fracture, and are apt to continue it in their minds in its due course as it should have been till turned adrift by the miscarriage, and until they can get a new hold to conduct them.[7]

[7] Ibid., 96.

Before considering North's formal attempts to define and classify music, we should like to note a remarkable passage in which he surveys the obstacles and limitations which are always conspiring to make great music making difficult.

> It is a greater undertaking to set forth a piece of music, than a poem, for that requires only the poet's wit and pains. But music demands not only utmost spirit and decorum in the composition, but little less than perfection in the performance, which is not always found; and the nicety in that quarter is such, that any miscarriage spoils the design. And diverse other mishaps poor music is liable to, as bad instruments, missing tune or time, and what is worst of all, the taste of the audience is commonly prejudicate and bizarre. Some affect one kind and will not bear another, and few allow any to be good that jumps not with their caprice.[8]

[8] Ibid., 70.

The core of North's definition of music, with respect to performance, is his classification of four types of music: solitary, social, ecclesiastical and theatrical. By solitary music he means the music one makes for oneself, either for amusement or for solace.

> With respect to amusement, and relief of an active mind distressed either with too much, or too little employment, nothing under the sun hath that virtue, as a solitary application to music. It is a medicine without any nausea or bitter, and is taken both for pleasure and cure.[9]

[9] Ibid., 257ff.

His most interesting comments on "social music" are relative to goals which the composer should attempt to achieve.

> People are apt to censure the whole according to the first and last relish.

......

> Whether the subject be merry or sad, the beginning of a work ought to be serious, and as much as may be majestic.

......

> There should be a continual regard to Humanity; for if there be in Nature any means to move the passions and affections, which were never denied to music, those ought to be pursued, as the best or rather the only means to please.

Church music, more than any kind of music, satisfied two of North's preferences—it was completely solemn ("all levities are excluded") and it was composed of a large sound, with an accompanied full chorus. Here, he says, "is a body of melody and harmony to fulfill the sharpest appetite to music." It is interesting that he also mentions the aesthetic advantage given the music by the architecture of the building in which it is performed.

North laments a serious shortage of singers available for church choirs and for this reason he recommends that perhaps the time has come to admit female singers into the choir.

> One might without a desperate solescisme maintain that if females were taken into the choirs instead of boys, it would be a vast improvement of choral music, because women come to a judgment as well as voice, which the boys's do not arrive at before their voices perish ... But both text[10] and morality are against it; and the Roman usage of castration is utterly unlawful, and a scandalous practice where it is used.

Regarding music for the theater, North objected to a tendency for melody to be common in style, vulgar he says, and because of the emphasis on melody the inner parts tended to have little purpose. This music, he says, should be left to its proper owners, the ordinary musicians. Such popular music "is most apt for driving away thinking, and letting in dancing."

North concludes his definition of music by adding that the two primary purposes of music are to please and to communicate emotions. In fact he makes three very important points here. First, he touches on the old harmony based

[10] I Corinthians 14:34:
> As in all the churches of the saints, the women should keep silence in the churches.

mathematical-polyphonic Church style verses the new humanistic emotional and melodic based new style. Second, he reminds his readers that the purpose of music is to communicate emotions. And third, equally important, that music has no *rational* purpose.

> Therefore in order to find the criteria of Good Music we must look into Nature itself, and the truth of things. Music hath two ends. First to please the sense, and that is done by the pure Dulcor of harmony, which is found chiefly in older music ... Secondly, to move the affections, or excite the passion; and that is done by measures of time joined with the former [the affections]. And it must be granted that pure impulse, artificially acted and continued, hath great power to excite men to act, but not to think.[11]

[11] Quoted in Wilson, *Roger North on Music*, 291ff.

He now expands on these ideas, beginning by returning to the point he wishes to stress about time and rhythm.

> I must sever the virtue of time in music, from the music itself, as having another scope and effect; and may be said to stir up comfortable actions, but not to excite thinking or please the sense.
>
> And as to all of music, besides the bare pleasing the sense, it must be referred to a power, by similar sounds, of bringing to our minds or memory the state of joy or grief, or of less important affections, as may be conform to what we hear. As for instance, who can hear the miserable clamor of one in affliction, without compassion? And whence that, but from a sensible reflection or memory of the same or like circumstances? And music by its sounds doth the same, and through the same operation of mind; for a savage, or brute, that hath no reflex thoughts, is not at all moved by compassionate sounds ... I have instanced grief, but the case is the same in all the various states of humanity; for by hearing certain sounds that are like what men commonly use by way of expressing their then present condition, our minds are affected accordingly ...
>
> But as to the point of better or worse intrinsically, reason may determine, but feeling [*humour*] must govern and pronounce. For the states of Humanity are infinitely various, and admit of all degrees of good and evil, important or frivolous, sane or distracted. And it must be granted that music which excites the best, most important and sane thinking and acting

is, in true judgment, the best music; and this will fall upon the ecclesiastical style ...

On the Purposes of Music

FOR NORTH, the central purpose and meaning of music, and consequently the core of his understanding of aesthetics in music, is its ability to communicate feeling. We understand today that it *is* the most important virtue of music, but, before the humanists began to think in these terms during the sixteenth century, this had been a concept opposed for one thousand years by the Church, and therefore for the entire early history of modern university study in music. While North is indebted to the earlier humanists, none of them expressed so clearly the dimension of this role of music.

> My thoughts are first in general that music is a true pantomime or resemblance of Humanity in all its states, actions, passions and affections. And in every musical attempt reasonably designed, Humane Nature is the subject ... so that an hearer shall put himself into the same condition, as if the state represented were his own ... So the melody should be referred to [man's] thoughts and affections. And an artist is to consider what manner of expression men would use on certain occasions, and let his melody, as near as may be, resemble that.[12]

[12] Quoted in Wilson, *Roger North on Music,* 110ff.

In vocal music North considers the matter of expressing emotions rather obvious, as they are contained in the words the singer sings—thus the singer is much to blame if he fails to express the proper emotions.[13] In objecting to "ridiculous absurdities" which result in some singers "humoring the words," North makes an important observation.

[13] Ibid., 112.

> For the sounds are not to represent the things commonly signified by words, but the thoughts of the person that uses them.[14]

[14] Ibid., 112ff.

He discounts most of what we call "text-painting" as something which corrupts music and as not reflecting what he means by expressing emotions.[15] Neither does merely the use of high or low pitches accomplish this. Because he finds some cantatas have lines more instrumental in character, he concludes that only singers should compose vocal music.[16]

The communication of specific emotions in instrumental music, because there are no words, North finds more difficult, indeed "we are much more at a loss than before."[17] In this case, he finds the composer has primarily two resources. The first is harmony, "which runs through the whole work and like the soul animates the mass ... therefore it is a chief care."

> The other is Humanity. I do not recollect any action of inanimates, and scarce of brutes, that can be brought under imitation in music, without relation to Humanity ...
>
> And here I must once for all observe that a fool can never be a good composer, nor a good painter. We do no mean of certain felicities that some derive from Nature, such as buffoonery and the like, but of reasonable invention; and who should ever be capable to represent anything, whereof he hath in his own mind no manner of Idea? Works of art in perfection do not come by accident but by design, though many times an happy conjuncture of the work and the spirits shall instill what may be called the sublime, at another time perhaps not to be reached; yet even that must fall under the correction of a good judgment, else it may prove *ignis fatuus* and good for nothing. Therefore a composer if he would not be counted a trifler, should understand the affairs of the world, and men; in a word, Humane Nature, with all its passions and affections, whereof in his compositions there must be found some sort of resemblance, as well as Harmony; as if he aimed to instruct, as well as to please ...
>
> And so music consists of harmony, and measure, which is called time. And in effect harmony works upon the thoughts, and the time upon the actions, of humane kind ... And it may be a rule, that no music can be well timed, that may not be danced, or with which men's actions may not conform.

We must regret that North did not dwell more on this last thought about the common ground between movement and music. We believed he seems to sense that movement is related to emotion as well

---

[15] In another place [Ibid., 266], North makes this point again and states that text-painting does not communicate emotions, because,

> ... having no relation to any state of humanity, such sounds lay hold of no passion ...

[16] Ibid., 113ff.
[17] Ibid., 115ff.

Next, North attempts to deal more specifically with emotions.[18]

[18] Ibid., 119ff.

> As for the passion of grief, it must be considered that every man living hath been sensible of it in himself, or in others, and acquainted with, or felt, the [mortal] occasions, and heard or made those dolorous cries that proceed from it ...

For such emotions, above, which he categorizes as "sedate griefs," one ordinarily uses the flat keys. However,

> the utterances of extreme pain, torture, or fright in any creature can never be represented in music, for they are always the worst of discord. But the extremes of joy and happiness are commonly expressed in the sharp keys, imitating trumpets and merry sings usual on such occasion; and all the dancing, theatrical, and festive music is chiefly of that kind.

He follows this with a very rare view of the familiar Italian words which refer only to tempo today, but originally carried more subjective meanings.

> But the hardest task is to square with a state either of business or of common conversation, unless the *Allemand* and *Fugue* do it. The *Adagios* are designed for pure and simple harmony, for which reason measure of time is so little regarded in them. The *Grave* comes nearer a sober conversation, and the *Allegro* light and chirping. The *Tremolo* is fear and suspicion, the *Andante* is a walking about full of concern, the *Ricercata* is a searching about for somewhat out of the way; the *Affectuoso* is expostulating, or *amour*; and so every other manner, as masters are pleased to title them, are but so many states of humane life, as they have a fancy to represent or imitate.

It is particularly interesting to find North again stressing the importance of the listener, assigning some responsibility to listener for the perception of the feelings expressed in the music. He finds it curious that he can find no research on this relationship, nor even important comment by earlier philosophers.

> If the listeners did not extend only their long ears to the entertainment in music, but a regulated understanding also, they would please themselves with exercising their critical

talents upon it, which scarcely any do now, but say only, This is very better, that worse. And they are very free of their tokens of rapture—very fine, great, stately, full, ayery, and such like indefinites—but not a wise word why or wherefore; all which a cat may pretend to as well as a man ... The study of this art hath enough to recommend it, being assisting to the composer and instructing to the hearers of music, and indeed adds a pleasure to life; for by all experience it is found, that no art gives equal pleasure to the ignorant and intelligent in it, but much the greatest share redounds to the latter.[19]

[19] Ibid., 124.

Another aspect fundamental to the listener, North finds, is acoustics. On this subject, in another place North suggests that the listener needs to be a certain distance from the music, although unfortunately he does not elaborate on this idea. It occurs to him as he is objecting to the difficulty the listener has in hearing fast, multi-part instrumental works such as fugues, or fugal allegros.

Perhaps an ear placed in the middle of the performers may distinguish somewhat, but at a decent position, the sum is a musical din, and no better; and music, like pictures, ought to have a just distance, or else the parts it consists of, which in all entertainments ought to be perceptible, will blend as in a mist.[20]

[20] Ibid., 189.

North now offers some observations on the communication of emotions in various forms. Church music he has observed can have such effect that the listeners find "they could not conceive any one nerve or vein in their whole body to be at rest."[21] Church music "being maintained in such a rigorous chastity, and ever serious ... [is] universally esteemed the best of music." Of operas, he observes,

[21] Ibid., 125ff.

There is certainly magnificence enough in them, and they may exhibit all the powers of Art, to move the audience ... There is nothing of music heretofore known among us, that ever matched the valuable part of our operas.

"Soft music," presumably some forms of chamber music, North has found does not move the listener as the larger church and opera forms. He seems to have experienced chamber music which mostly entertained the listener, but not moved him.

> Soft music is also useful in a private application, as to dispose great persons to rest, and thereby laudable beyond imagination; so also chamber entertainments, and decoration of a song, or at a levee, are all very good, and may please, but not ravish.

But, anything which centers on entertainment, fails, in North's view, to achieve the higher purpose of music.

> Lord! how at the wagging of an elbow the whole theater claps, though no single note is heard: just like a circle of fools laughing at the wagging of a feather, such power hath ignorance and partiality. I would go to such music and pay my scott as I do to the posture man, or a rope dancer, to see somewhat done which I scarce thought possible. But if I went for the sake of the music in earnest, it should be to feel my spirits moved, and together with the delightful sounds, enjoy the gentle enlivenings of passions, which ... may justly be accounted the best of human life.[22]

[22] Ibid., 129.

Going beyond the communication of emotions, North seemed to believe with the ancient Greeks that music had the ability to affect character, something no doubt he arrived at primarily from his own amateur music making in the home. Unfortunately he does not elaborate on this, taking instead an easier path by making observations on the secondary effect of music. North reflects on the early days of the seventeenth century when amateur music making in the country homes of the upper class flourished. He saw a link between the rising professional level of performance, and the consequent centering of performance in London, with the decline of the earlier amateur tradition. Taking music out of the home, in his view, created the opportunity for a decline in morals.

> And this is done by observing that vice will start up to fill the vacancy. When we know not how to pass the time, we fall to drink. If company is not at home, we go out to markets and meetings to find such as will join in debauchery. There can scarce be a full family kept, because this humor of drunkening

let in all manner of lewdness. Even fathers and daughters, with servants and children male and female, go into promiscuousness. And it is scarce reasonable to expect better unless you can provide diversion, to fill the time of the less employed part of a gentile family ... By this you may judge what profit the public hath from the improvement of music. I am almost of Plato's opinion, that the state ought to govern the use of it.[23]

[23] Ibid., 11ff.

14
Bacon on Music

FRANCIS BACON (1561–1626) was referred to by Will Durant as "the greatest and proudest intellect of the age" and Durant places him at the head of the Age of Reason.[1] If he were not the inventor of inductive reasoning (the study of nature through experience and experiment) as he is often credited, he may at least be credited with being one of those who popularized the scientific method. His quest for knowledge through experimentation caused his death when his attempt to forestall putrefaction in a fowl with ice led to a fever.

Bacon, son of a high government official, served in Parliament, was a successful lawyer and eventually held important government posts himself. Unfortunately he was prone to bribes, participated in corruption and was eventually sent to prison in the Tower.

Bacon's basic ideas on the nature of the organization of man and his mind are expressed in his *The Advancement of Learning*. Man's understanding, he says, is the seat of learning and has three divisions: Memory, taught through history; Imagination, taught through poetry; and Reason, taught through philosophy.[2] The study of History he divides into Natural, Civil and Ecclesiastical. Of these three we are most interested in the history of Nature, for this he further subdivides into the three divisions of Creatures, Marvels and the Arts.[3]

[1] Will Durant, *The Age of Reason Begins* (New York: Simon and Schuster, 1961), 169, 183.

[2] *The Advancement of Learning*, in *The Works of Francis Bacon*, ed. James Spedding (Cambridge: Cambridge University Press, 1869), VI, 182,

[3] Ibid., VI, 184.

As for the study of human knowledge itself, Bacon states that it consists of two fields: the study of the substance of the soul or mind itself and the study of the functions of its faculties.[4] As for the first of these, Bacon finds that all previous attempts to explain the soul leave one "in a maze." Since the soul is a divine gift, therefore, he concludes, it can only be understood by divine inspiration and is not a subject for philosophy.

Turning to that which can be studied, Bacon comes tantalizingly close to deducing the basic operation of the brain by finding it divided into Understanding and Reason on one hand, and Appetite and Emotion on the other.[5] He then adds a faculty of Imagination, independent of either and through which both Reason and the Emotions operate.

We find it curious that Bacon reverts to the medieval Church dogma which attributed no value to personal experience. Bacon finds the knowledge gained from personal experience to be that of "false appearances," as compared to reality.[6] In other words, he fails to perceive the understanding gained by personal experience is valid and important, for it is this which distinguishes the individual. In another place, however, he gives quite a contrary assessment of experiential knowledge.

> The knowledge of man is as the waters, some descending from above, and some springing from beneath; the one informed by the light of nature, the other inspired by divine revelation. The light of nature consists in the notions of the mind and the reports of the senses; for as for knowledge which man receives by teaching, it is cumulative and not original.[7]

Bacon also writes of the danger which the emotions represent to Reason and in fact suggests that man is only able to function rationally because imagination forms a "confederacy" with Reason against the emotions.[8] He admits the emotions, like Reason, are capable of good, but finds this distinction:

> Emotion beholds merely the present; reason beholds the future and sum of time.[9]

[4] Ibid., VI, 254ff.

[5] Ibid., 258ff. He finds Reason has four separate faculties: those to invent, to seek, to judge and to communicate.

[6] Ibid., 278.

[7] Ibid., 207.

[8] Ibid., 299.

[9] Ibid.

It fails to occur to him that this is one of the great virtues of music, that it communicates with the listener in the present tense, whereas the entire world of the intellect is past tense by its very definition.

In another place he speaks of the danger by which the emotions threaten Reason by using the analogy of the afflictions of the body and again with the analogy of the wind which stirs up the calm waters of the ocean.[10] Finally, he concludes,

[10] Ibid., 336.

> The poets and writers of histories are the best doctors of this knowledge; where we may find painted forth with great life, how emotions are kindled and incited; and how pacified and reframed ... how they work, how they vary, how they gather and fortify, how they are enwrapped one within another, and how they do fight and encounter one with another ...

Later he makes a statement which reminds us of the basic attitude of some American university music departments toward musical performance.

> In the mind whatsoever knowledge reason cannot at all work upon and convert, is mere intoxication, and endangers a dissolution of the mind and understanding.[11]

[11] Ibid., 404.

In Book Eight of his Natural History, Bacon discusses the physical effects of the passions on the body. Here he includes fear, joy, anger, light displeasure, shame, wonder, laughing, lust and grief and pain.

> Grief and pain cause sighing, sobbing, groaning, screaming and roaring, tears, distorting of the face, grinding of the teeth, sweating. Sighing is caused by the drawing in of a greater quantity of breath to refresh the heart that labors; like a great draught when one is thirsty. Sobbing is the same thing stronger ... Tears are caused by a contraction of the spirits of the brain; which contraction by consequence astringeth the moisture of the brain, and thereby sends tears into the eyes.[12]

[12] *Natural History,* Century VIII, Section 714.

In Bacon's *History of Life and Death*, he discusses the emotions from the perspective of their physical influence on the body. Among his more interesting contentions, we find,

> Great joys attenuate and diffuse the spirits, and shorten life; ordinary cheerfulness strengthens the spirits ...
>
> Sensual impressions of joys are bad ...
>
> Joy suppressed and sparingly communicated comforts the spirits more than joy indulged and published.[13]
>
> Grief and sadness, if devoid of fear, and not too keen, rather prolong life ... [14]
>
> Great fears shorten life.
>
> Suppressed anger is a kind of vexation, and makes the spirit to prey upon the juices of the body.
>
> Envy is the worst of passions, and preys on the spirits ...
>
> A light shame hurts not, because it slightly contracts the spirits and then diffuses them ...
>
> Love, if not unfortunate, and too deeply wounding, is a kind of joy ...
>
> Hope is of all the emotions the most useful, and contributes most to prolong life ... [15]

Bacon correctly observes that the motions of the face "disclose the present humor and state of the mind and will."[16] For this reason, in another place he recommends that one maintain a "steadfast countenance, not wavering, etc., in conversation."[17]

Bacon's observations on Beauty are limited to physical beauty, but we like his comment, "Virtue is nothing but inward beauty; beauty nothing but outward virtue."[18] In his essay, "on Beauty," he does digress once to the subject of painters. Painters, he observes, could paint a face on the basis of geometrical proportions, or by taking the best parts of many models, but it would always be the case that no one but the painter would like them. It is also interesting here that in order to explain that a good painter must rely on inspiration instead of rules, he turns to music as an analogy.

> Not but I think a painter may make a better face than ever was; but he must do it by a kind of felicity (as a musician makes an excellent melody in music) and not by rule. A man shall see faces, that if you examine them part by part, you shall find never a good; and yet altogether do well.[19]

Bacon's only important reflection on drama seems to suggest that he saw its primary purpose as one of education,

---

[13] Later [*History of Life and Death*, in Ibid., X, 144], he states that sudden grief or fear can produce sudden death. In addition, "Many have died from great and sudden joys."

[14] In his "Medical Remains" [Ibid., VII, 424], Bacon offers the recipe for making a "wine against adverse melancholy, preserving the senses and the reason." This involves roots of bugloss, misted with wine containing three ounces of refined gold, etc.

[15] *History of Life and Death*, in Ibid., X, 98ff.

[16] *The Advancement of Learning*, in Ibid., VI, 238.

[17] "Civil Conversation," in Ibid., XIII, 309.

[18] Ibid., IX, 156.

[19] "Of Beauty," in Ibid., XII, 226.

but again he had to turn to an analogy with music to explain how drama affects the mind. We might add that we regard his final sentence here as being very near what should be the heart of music education.

> Dramatic Poetry, which has the theater for its world, would be of excellent use if well directed. For the stage is capable of no small influence both of discipline and of corruption. Now of corruptions in this kind we have enough; but the discipline has in our times been plainly neglected. And though in modern states play-acting is esteemed but as a toy, except when it is too satirical and biting; yet among the ancients it was used as a means of educating men's minds to virtue. Nay, it has been regarded by learned men and great philosophers as a kind of musician's bow by which men's minds may be played upon. And certainly it is most true, and one of the great secrets of nature, that the minds of men are more open to impressions and emotions when many are gathered together than when they are alone.[20]

While Bacon was obviously much interested in music, he rarely writes of its fundamental definition. In his *The Advancement of Learning*, he seems to reflect the old Scholastic definition that music is one of a series of studies dependent on mathematics.[21] Perhaps his most interesting remarks on this subject are found in his *Sapientia Veterum*:

> For it seems there are two kinds of harmony and music; one of divine providence, the other of human reason; and to the human judgment, and the ears as it were of mortals, the government of the world and nature, and the more secret judgments of God, sound somewhat harsh and untunable; and though this be ignorance, such as deserves to be distinguished with the ears of an ass, yet those ears are worn secretly and not in the face of the world—for it is not a thing observed or noted as a deformity by the vulgar.[22]

Bacon concludes his discussion of music in his *Natural History* by presenting, without discussion, the categories under which music might be discussed. We particularly wish he might have elaborated on number five. Had he done so, music education today might be quite different in nature.

[20] *The Advancement of Learning*, Book II, in Ibid., VIII, 441ff.

[21] *The Advancement of Learning*, in Ibid., VI, 227.

[22] *De Sapientia Veterum*, in Ibid., XIII, 100.

1. Musical, unmusical
2. Treble, bass
3. Flat, sharp
4. Soft, loud
5. Exterior, interior
6. Clean, harsh or purling
7. Articulate, inarticulate.

On the Perception of Music

Bacon devotes Book Two of his *Natural History* to considerations on the nature of music and sound. His inspiration seems to have been his thought that the quality of the intellectual discussion of the theories behind music did not equal the significance of the performance with which he was familiar.

> Music, in the practice, hath been well pursued and in good variety; but in the theory, and especially in the yielding of the causes of the practice, very weakly; begin reduced into certain mystical subtleties, of no use and not much truth.[23]

[23] *Natural History*, Section 101.

Unfortunately, much of Bacon's speculation on the nature of sound and music is based on a faulty understanding of the physics of sound, as, indeed, the conclusions of most early writers were. Simply put, early writers did not understand that the sound we hear is vibrations created by a string or an instrument, etc. However, Bacon comes close when he states "The sound is not created between the bow and the string; but between the string and the air." He believed the musical instrument set in motion something he called "local motion," and it was here the sound was created. His clearest explanation reads,

> It would be extreme grossness to think that the sound in strings is made or produced between the hand and the strings, or the quill and the string, or the bow and the string, for those are but *vehicula motus*, passages to the creation of the sound;

the sound being produced between the string and the air; and that not by any impulsion of the air from the first motion of the string, by the return or result of the string, which was strained by the touch, to his former place; which motion of result is quick and sharp; whereas the first motion is soft and dull. So the bow tortures the string continually, and therefore holds it in a continual trepidation.[24]

[24] Ibid., Section 137.

Failing to perceive the true nature of vibrations, Bacon is led to a number of curious conclusions. Since he regarded that the sound is created in the air immediately surrounding the instrument, it seemed to him that a particular force was necessary to set this air in motion, as one could clearly see in wind players.

> For as for other wind instruments, they require a forcible breath; as trumpets, cornets, hunters' horns, etc., which appeareth by the blown cheeks of him that windeth them.[25]

[25] Ibid., Section 116.

All pipes, he says, have "a blast, as well as a sound." Even speech, he concluded, results from the "expulsion of a little breath."[26] This explosion of air which he associates with tone production leads him to an extraordinary observation,

[26] Ibid., Section 125.

> It hath been anciently reported, and is still received, that extreme applause and shouting of people assembled in great multitudes, have so rarefied and broken the air, that birds flying over have fallen down, the air being not able to support them.[27]

[27] Ibid., Section 127.

Since Bacon understood music to be created in the air, and not in the vibrations, he was at a loss to explain why vibrating tongs set in water seem to produce sounds under water where there is no air present.[28] He also appears to have been somewhat mystified by the existence of echoes. If it were a *real* [corporeal] sound, then the echo would have to have been produced in a similar fashion as the original sound, that is by a violin string, a trumpet tone, etc. Since this is obviously not the case, Bacon took the echo to be "a great argument for the spiritual essence of sounds."[29]

[28] Ibid., Section 133.

[29] Ibid., Section 287.

Failing to understand the nature of vibrations led to a number of other curious conclusions. To his ear, the bass was

generally stronger than the treble. From this perception he makes this contention:

> In harmony, if there be not a discord to the bass, it doth not disturb the harmony though there be a discord to the higher parts ... And the cause is, for that the bass striking more air, doth overcome and drown the treble (unless the discord be very odious); and so hideth a small imperfection.[30]

[30] Ibid., Section 109.

Similarly, he adds, but cannot explain, that stopping high on a string not only produces a high pitch, but a dull sound.[31] His failure to understand the true nature of vibrations leads him to strange explanations:

[31] Ibid., Section 156.

> The loudness and softness of sounds is a thing distinct from the magnitude and exility of sounds; for a bass string, though softly struck, gives the greater sound; but a treble string, if hard struck, will be heard much further off. And the cause is, for that the bass string strikes more air; and the treble less air, but with a sharper percussion.[32]

[32] Ibid., Section 163.

On the subject of acoustics, again failing an understanding of overtones, Bacon arrives at curious explanations for the differing sounds of instruments.

> All instruments that have either returns, as trumpets; or flexions, as cornets; or are drawn up and put from, as sackbuts; have a purling sound: but the recorder or flute, that have none of these inequalities, give a clear sound. Nevertheless, the recorder itself, or pipe, moistened a little in the inside, sounds more solemnly, and with a little purling or hissing.[33]

[33] Ibid., Section 170.

Bacon touches on acoustics again in his fictional, *New Atlantis*. Among his descriptions of various civic buildings in this utopian town, there is an extraordinary suggestion for a kind of experimental acoustic studio.

> We have also sound-houses, where we practice and demonstrate all sounds and their generation. We have harmony which you have not, of quarter-sounds and lesser slides of sounds. Diverse instruments of music likewise to you unknown, some sweeter than any you have; with bells and rings that are dainty and sweet. We represent small sounds as great and deep, likewise great sounds extenuate and sharp; we

make diverse tremblings and warblings of sounds, which in their original are entire. We represent and imitate all articulate sounds and letters, and the voices and notes of beasts and birds. We have certain helps which, set to the ear, do further the hearing greatly; we have also diverse strange and artificial echoes, reflecting the voice many times, and, as it were, tossing it; and some that give back the voice louder than it came, some shriller and some deeper, yea some rendering the voice, differing in the letters or articulate sound from that they receive. We have all means to convey sounds in trunks and pipes, in strange lines and distances.[34]

[34] *New Atlantis*, in Ibid., V, 407.

In an attempt to explain what aesthetic principles result in the "pleasing" quality in music, Bacon looked for correspondence with the sense of sight. In his *Natural History*, the element of "pleasing" in sight, he found, is in that which has equality, good proportion or correspondence and these he considered identical with music. In addition, he offers a comment on vibrato,

> The division and quavering, which please so much in music, have an agreement with the glittering of light; as the moonbeams playing upon a wave.[35]

[35] *Natural History*, Section 111, 113.

He also briefly points to the correspondence between music and oratory, suggesting that imitation and fugal writing can be equated to repetition and traduction in rhetoric.

Returning to his comparison of sight and hearing, Bacon notes that the eye sees a vast panorama of objects, keeping them all separate, whereas this is not pleasing with respect to sound.

> The sweetest and best harmony is, when every part or instrument is not heard by itself, but a conflation of them all; which requires one to stand some distance off.[36]

[36] Ibid., Section 224ff.

Bacon also observes that "some consorts of instruments are sweeter than others," but this is, he says, "a thing not sufficiently yet observed."[37]

[37] Ibid., Section 278.

Next Bacon offers a variety of observations regarding the most pleasing sounds obtainable from various instruments. A pipe, he maintains, if moist inside, but without actual drops of water, sounds "a more solemn sweet" than if dry.[38] Music sounds better indoors during frosty weather. If one sings into the hole of a drum, it makes the singing sweeter. This leads him to an unusual suggestion for choral performance:

> And so I conceive it would, if it were a song in parts, sung into several drums; and for the handsomeness and strangeness sake, it would not be amiss to have a curtain between the place where the drums are and the listeners.

[38] Ibid., Section 230ff. In his "Physiological Remains," however, Bacon says of bells,
> It is probable that it is the dryness of the metal that helps the clearness of the sound, and the moistness that dulls it. [Ibid., VII, 389]

Bacon observes that sounds are better if one's mind is concentrated on only one sense, hearing. Therefore he suggests that music sounds better at night than during the day.[39]

Bacon is skeptical in his two brief references to the "Music of the Spheres," a topic still much discussed by philosophers and astronomers, in particular by Kepler.

> The heavens turn about in a most rapid motion, without noise to us perceived; though in some dreams they have been said to make an excellent music.[40]

[39] Bacon also mentions in passing [Ibid., Section 241] the subject of "counterfeiting the distance of voices." But he sees no purpose for this, other than for "imposture, in counterfeiting ghosts or spirits."

[40] Ibid., Section 115.

In a catalog of projected histories, Bacon includes an "History of Sounds in the upper region (if there be any)."[41]

Finally, we might mention that in his *History of Dense and Rare*, Bacon, while discussing "motion of dilatation and contraction in the air by heat," mentions without further identification a musical instrument "played by the rays of the sun."[42]

[41] "Catalog of Particular Histories," in Ibid., VIII, 374.

[42] *History of Dense and Rare*, in Ibid., X, 265.

On the Purpose of Music

Bacon passes by the usual discussion on the purposes of music for pleasure and to solace the listener in preference to concentrating on its direct physical affect. In particular, his focus is the ancient belief of ethos and he exhibits an enthusiasm rarely found among modern philosophers.

> It has been anciently held and observed, that the sense of hearing and the kinds of music most in operation upon manners; as to encourage men and make them warlike; to make them soft and effeminate; to make them grave; to make

them light; to make them gentle and inclined to pity; etc. The cause is, for that the sense of hearing strikes the spirits more immediately than the other senses, and more incorporeally than the smelling. For the sight, taste, and feeling, have their organs not of so present and immediate access to the spirits, as the hearing has. And as for the smelling (which indeed works also immediately upon the spirits, and is forcible while the object remains), it is with a communication of the breath or vapor of the object odorate; but harmony, entering easily, and mingling not at all, and coming with a manifest motion, doth by custom of often affecting the spirits and putting them into one kind of posture, alter not a little the nature of the spirits, even when the object is removed. And therefore we see that tunes and airs, even in their own nature, have in themselves some affinity with the affections: as there be merry tunes, doleful tunes, solemn tunes; tunes inclining men's minds to pity; warlike tunes, etc. So as it is no marvel if they alter the spirits, considering that tunes have a predisposition to the motion of the spirits in themselves. But yet it hath been noted, that though this variety of tunes disposes the spirits to variety of passions conform unto them, yet generally music feeds that disposition of the spirits which it finds. We see also that several airs and tunes do please several nations and persons, according to the sympathy they have with their spirits.[43]

[43] *Natural History*, Section 114.

On this general subject, Bacon also makes a very interesting comment touching on music therapy.

This variable composition of man's body has made it as an instrument easy to distemper; and therefore the poets did well to conjoin Music and Medicine in Apollo: because the office of medicine is but to tune this curious harp of Man's body and to reduce it to harmony.[44]

[44] *The Advancement of Learning*, in Ibid., VI, 242.

15
Milton on Music

Where no arts flourish, where all knowledge is banished, where indeed there is no trace of a good man, there savageness and frightful barbarism rage about... Europe, from the whole of which during several early centuries all good arts had perished; for a long time the presiding Muses had abandoned all the universities of that age: blind Ignorance had pervaded and taken possession of everything; nothing was heard in the schools except the absurd dogmas of most stupid monks.[1]

Milton

[1] "Prolusions," in *The Works of John Milton*, ed. Frank Patterson (New York: Columbia University Press, 1931–1938), XII, 259.

JOHN MILTON (1608–1674) is considered by the English to be their greatest poet after Shakespeare. His cultural development began in childhood due to unusually active parents, his father being a legal writer and musician and his mother an activist in charitable causes. He tells us that his early studies included music.

I gave myself up entirely to reading the Greek and Latin writers; exchanging, however, sometimes, the country for the town, either for the purchase of books, or to learn something new in mathematics, or in music, which at the time furnished the sources of my amusement.[2]

[2] "A Second Defence of the English People," Ibid., VIII, 121.

A later comment suggests that this early experience in music may have helped determine that his path was to be poetry and literature.

... amid the rugged difficulties of the Arts, that having lost all hope of obtaining quiet, I began to think sorrowfully ... that it would be better to forget the Arts completely.³

[3] "Prolusions," in Ibid., XII, 251.

His formal studies in England included extensive readings in the literature of the major European countries, in addition to expanding the religious studies which had begun in his strongly Puritan home. His studies completed, his generous father enabled Milton to tour France and Italy. He was particularly taken by Italy, which he called "the retreat of civility and of all polite learning,"⁴ and while there met a number of literati, including the aged Galileo.

[4] "A Second Defence of the English People," in Ibid., VIII, 115.

As a Puritan, Milton fully shared the old Catholic view that Reason must rule man's activities.

> But know that in the Soul
> Are many lesser Faculties that serve
> Reason as chief; among these Fancy next
> Her office holds; of all external things,
> Which the five watchful Senses represent,
> She forms Imaginations, Aerie shapes,
> Which Reason joining or disjoining, frames
> All what we affirm or what deny ...⁵

[5] "Paradise Lost," V, 100ff, in Ibid., II, 147.

And he agreed with the old Church that the support of Reason was a primary church concern. "The Church," he maintained, "hath in her immediate care those inner parts and affections of the mind where the seat of reason is."⁶ This was, of course, due to constant competition between Reason and the emotions for the possession of man. "Take heed," warns Milton, "least Passion sway thy Judgment."⁷

[6] "Church-Government," in Ibid., III, 182.

[7] "Paradise Lost," VIII, 635, in Ibid., II, 258.

Milton did not seem to recognize the emotions as an entirely separate faculty apart from Reason and it is curious that he even associates laughter primarily with Reason: "every man is able to laugh because he is rational."⁸ His most direct definition of the emotions in general is merely a restatement of views of older writers.

[8] "The Art of Logic," I, iii, in Ibid., XI, 31. In another place, he says both anger and laughter are "rational" faculties. ["Animadversions," in Ibid., III, 108]

> The affections are love, hatred; joy, sorrow; hope, fear; and anger.
> Love is to be so regulated, that our highest affections may be placed on the objects most worthy of them ...⁹

[9] "The Christian Doctrine," in Ibid., XVII, 203.

Milton's most interesting comments relative to Art in general are centered in the perception of Art and in related educational aspects. We are not surprised, in view of his comments on the association of the emotions with the intellect, to find him writing, "The perception of all art and of all science concerns only the intellect."[10] On the other hand, in another place he refers to the old Scholastic distinction between the "speculative" and the practice of art and here he leans more toward the practical rather than the conceptual.

[10] "Prolusions," in Ibid., XII, 261.

> For as none can judge of a painter, or a sculpturer but he who is an artist, that is, either in the *Practice* or the *Theory*, which is often separated from practice, and judges learnedly without it ...[11]

[11] "An Apology," in Ibid., III, 346.

Milton does not discuss in detail any of the traditional topics associated with the philosophy of aesthetics in the arts. He discusses Beauty only with respect to women, although he does create a memorable phrase: "Beauty is nature's coin."[12]

[12] "A Mask," in Ibid., I, 112ff.

In the preface to "Paradise Lost," Milton disparages contemporary English theater.

> Not without cause therefore some both Italian and Spanish poets of prime note have rejected rhyme both in longer and shorter works, as have also our best English Tragedies, as a thing of itself, to all judicious ears, trivial and of no true musical delight ...[13]

[13] "Paradise Lost," in Ibid., II, 6.

We must also note Milton's comment that "the frequenting of Theaters against her husbands mind" is sufficient cause for divorce.[14]

[14] "Divorce," in Ibid., III, 487.

As we have noted above Milton was born into a musical family and enjoyed some study of music during his youth. If he did not continue as an active performer, his appreciation of music remained and his poetry is full of reference to it. Consider this remarkable tribute:

> Do not look down on song divine, creation of the bard, for naught graces more finely than does song his heavenly source, his heavenly seed, his mind mortal in origin, for song still keeps holy traces of Prometheus's fire. The gods above love

song, and song has power to rouse the quaking depths of Tartarus, to bind fast the gods of the deeps below; song restrains with triple adamant the unfeeling [men]. By song the secrets of the far-distant future are revealed by the daughters of Phoebus, and by quivering Sibyls, pale of lips. The sacrificer composes songs at the holy alters ... I too shall go, wearing a golden crown, through the realms of the skies, wedding sweet strains to the soft-sounding plectrum ...[15]

[15] "Ad Patrem," in Ibid., I, 271.

We know some of his tastes, as for example this comment which follows a reference to the loud trumpet in one poem:

Me softer airs befit, and softer strings
Of Lute, or Viol still, more apt for mournful things.[16]

[16] "The Passion," in Ibid., I, 24.

And we know one of his preferences among composers, as we see in a sonnet in praise of the songs of the English composer, Henry Lawes.

Harry whose tuneful and well measured Song
First taught our English Musick how to span
Words with just note and accent ...[17]

[17] "To Mr. H. Lawes, on his Aires," in Ibid., I, 63.

We can also see the extent of Milton's familiarity with music in his frequent use of various aspects of music in his figures of speech. He uses "harmony" to represent aspects of social order, a metaphor which had been popular with the ancient Greeks. In his treatise on church government, for example, it stands for the discipline needed in social organization.

Nor is there any sociable perfection in this life civil or sacred that can be above discipline, but she is that which with her musical chords preserves and holds all the parts thereof together.[18]

[18] "Church-Government," in Ibid., III, 185.

He even uses this metaphor when writing on the subject of divorce.

Nature, from whence are derived the issues of love and hatred distinctly flowing through the whole mass of created things, and that God's doing ever is to bring the due likenesses and harmonies of his works together, except when out of two contraries meet to their own destruction ...[19]

[19] "Divorce," in Ibid., III, 418.

Similarly, harmony is a metaphor for the relationship between two persons.

> For I no sooner in my Heart divined,
> My Heart, which by a secret harmonie
> Still moves with thine, joined in connection sweet ... [20]

[20] "Paradise Lost," X, 357ff, in Ibid., VIII, 53.

He uses the organ to represent one who stimulates others to action.

> As in an Organ from one blast of wind
> To many a row of Pipes the sound-board breathes.[21]

[21] "Paradise Lost," I, 708, in Ibid., II, 33.

Music is, of course, the most satisfactory symbol for feeling and is one often used by Milton. A poignant example is his use of a musical metaphor to express his sadness in thinking of the death of Jesus.

> For now to sorrow must I tune my song,
> And set my Harp to notes of saddest woe ... [22]

[22] "The Passion," in Ibid., I, 23.

In his "Second Defence of the English Peoples," after a discussion of King Charles, Milton uses the loud trumpeter as a metaphor for a critic.

> Having thus dispatched Charles, he is now preparing, with no little blustering, his attack upon me: "After these preludes, the wonderful Salmasius will blow the terrible trumpet." You prognosticate health, and give us notice of a new king of musical harmony: for when that terrible trumpet shall be blown, we can think of no fitter accompaniment for it than a reiterated crepitation. But I would advise Salmasius not to inflate his cheek overmuch: for you may take my word for it, that the more it is swollen out, the fairer will he present it for slaps, in musical response, while both his cheeks ring again, to this modulated tone of the wonderful Salmasius ... [23]

[23] "A Second Defence of the English People," in Ibid., VIII, 53.

Milton also made numerous historical references to music, beginning with the Greek myths where he finds the gods "contended only for beauty, or in music."[24] Milton was wrong in fact, but perhaps current in Puritan thought, when he described ancient man as having no music of any kind, "when suddenly Arts and Sciences divinely inspired the rude hearts of men."[25]

[24] Ibid., VIII, 193.

[25] "Prolusions," VII, in Ibid., XII, 273.

In a letter, he mentioned the public musical entertainments of "truly Roman magnificence" given by Cardinal Barberini,[26] and in his "Commonplace Book," Milton makes an interesting comment on even earlier Roman musical history. Ignatius, the third bishop of Antioch after Peter, he reports, was the first to devise antiphonal singing in the church. The organ he says was first introduced to France by ambassadors of the Byzantine Emperor, Constantine V, who brought organs to King Pepin.[27]

With respect to the early music history of his own country, Milton mentions Begabredus, who "is recorded to have excelled all before him in the Art of Music,"[28] and contends that it was the Saxons under whom the liberal arts, including music, first flourished.[29] We wish for more detail, when he mentions that King Alfred disguised himself as a musician and, by playing his lute and singing, functioned as a spy.[30]

[26] "Familiar Letters," in Ibid., XII, 41.

[27] "To Leonora, as She Sings at Rome," in Ibid., I, 229.

[28] "De Musica," in Ibid., XVIII, 140.

[29] Ibid., 169.

[30] "History of Britain," in Ibid., X, 234.

On the Perception of Music

Milton's only emphatic comment on the perception of music is that variety is crucial.

> Variety (as both Musick and Rhethorick teacheth us) erects and rouses an Auditory, like the masterful running over many chords and divisions; whereas if men should ever be thumming the drone of one plain song, it would be a dull opiate to the most wakeful attention.[31]

[31] "Animadversions," in Ibid., III, 133.

We feel we must include here the obvious attention which Milton devoted to the question of the Music of the Spheres. He mentions this frequently in his poetry, beginning with the music of creation.

> ... up he rode
> Followed with acclamation and the sound
> Symphonious of ten thousand Harps that tuned
> Angelic harmonies: the Earth, the Air
> Resounded, (thou remember'st, for thou heardst)
> The Heavens and all the Constellations rung,
> The Planets in their station listening stood ...[32]

[32] "Paradise Lost," VII, 557, in Ibid., II, 231. In the same poem [V, 178] there is a reference to stars that move "in mystic Dance not without Song."

Several poems speak of the music of the spheres being in nine-parts, representing the seven known planets, the sun and our moon. In the poem, "The Hymn," we find,

> Ring out ye Crystal spheres,
> Once bless our humane ears,
> (If ye have power to touch our senses so)
> And let your silver chime
> Move in melodious time;
> And let the Base of Heavens deep Organ blow,
> And with your ninefold harmony
> Make up full consort to the Angelike symphony.[33]

[33] "The Hymn," in Ibid., I, 6.

And again in "Arcades":

> But else in deep of night when drowsiness
> Hath locked up mortal sense, then listen I
> To the celestial Sirens harmony,
> That sit upon the nine enfolded Spheres ... [34]

[34] "Arcades," in Ibid., I, 74.

Why, even God listens to the music of the spheres.

> And in their motions harmonie Divine
> So smooths her charming tones, that Gods own ear
> Listens delighted.[35]

[35] "Paradise Lost," in V, 625ff, Ibid., II, 166.

In several places, such as in his masque composed for a performance at Ludlow Castle in 1634, Milton refers to the music of the spheres as "the Starry Quire."[36] One of these "starry choir" references provides the only attempt by Milton to portray the actual music, "a never-dying melody, a song beyond all describing."[37]

[36] "A Masque," in Ibid., I, 89. A song in this masque also mentions "all Heaven's Harmonies." [Ibid., I, 94].

[37] "Ad Patrem," line 35.

Eventually, Milton contributes a lengthy discussion, "On the Music of the Spheres," which appears to be intended to be used in a lecture called "In the Public Schools." Milton is suspicious, but he seems to leave open the possibility of the music of the spheres. He wonders, how can we be expected to hear this music of the heavens, since our concerns are so earth-bound.

> If there is any place for a man of my poor powers, fellow students, after so many speakers of consequence have been heard today, I shall attempt even at this moment to express,

in accordance with my small ability, how well I wish the established exercise of the present occasion; and I shall follow, albeit far outdistanced, in the course of this day's demonstration of eloquence. Accordingly, while I avoid and shun entirely those common and ordinary topics of discourse, the purpose of this day and likewise of those who, I suspected, would speak appropriately concerning matters fitted to the time, kindles and straightaway rouses my mind to attempt with ardor some new theme. These two reasons are able to furnish incentives or keenness to one somewhat sluggish and for the most part possessed of a dull wit. Wherefore, a few words at least suggest themselves to be pronounced, as they say, with open hand and with rhetorical embellishment, about that famous heavenly harmony, concerning which very shortly there is to be a disputation with the closed fist; consideration of the time being observed, which now presses me on and restrains me. I would prefer, however that you, my hearers, should regard these things as said in jest.

For what sane man would have thought that Pythagoras, that god of the philosophers, at whose name all mortals of his age stood up in very sacred veneration;—who, I say, would have thought that he would ever have expressed in public an opinion so uncertainly founded? Surely, if indeed he taught the harmony of the spheres and that the heavens revolved with melodious charm, he wished to signify by it, in his wise way, the very loving and affectionate relations of the orbs and their eternally uniform revolutions according to the fixed laws of necessity. Certainly, in this he imitated either the poets or, what is almost the same thing, the divine oracles, by whom no secret and hidden mystery is exhibited in public, unless clad in some covering or garment. That most skillful interpreter of Mother Nature, Plato, has followed him, since he affirms that certain sirens sit one upon each of the circles of the heavens and hold spell-bound gods and men by their most honey-sweet song. And finally, this agreement of things universal and this loving concord, which Pythagoras secretly introduced in poetic fashion by the term Harmony, Homer likewise suggested significantly and appropriately by means of that famous golden chain of Jove hanging down from heaven.

Aristotle, the envious and perpetual calumniator of Pythagoras and Plato, desiring to pave a way to renown on the shattered opinions of these great men, imputed to Pythagoras the unheard symphony of the heavens and tunes of the spheres. But if either fate or necessity had decreed that your soul, O Father Pythagoras, should have been translated into me, there would not have been lacking one who would easily have come to your rescue, however great the infamy under which you were laboring at the moment. Indeed, why should not the celestial bodies during their everlasting courses evolve musical sounds? Does it not seem fair to you, O Aristotle? Truly, I hardly believe your intelligences would be able to endure with patience that sedentary toil of the rolling heavens for so many ages, unless that ineffable song of the stars had prevented your departure and by the charm of its melody had persuaded a delay. It would be as if you were to take away from heaven those beautiful little goddesses and should deliver the ministering gods to mere drudgery and to condemn them to the treadmill. Nay indeed, Atlas himself long ago would have withdrawn his shoulders from a heaven that was about to fall, had not that sweet song soothed, with its most delightful charm, him, gasping and sweating under his great burden. In addition to these things the Dolphin, wearied of his constellation, would long ago have preferred his own seas to heaven, if he had not rightly been burning with the thought that the singing orbs of the sky excelled by far the sweetness of Arion's lyre. Why, credible it is that the lark itself should fly right up to the clouds at early dawn, and that the nightingale should spend the whole lonely night in song, in order that they may adjust their strains to the harmonic mode of the sky, to which they listen attentively. Thus also from the very beginning of things the story has prevailed about the Muses dancing day and night around the altar of Jove; hence from remote antiquity skill with the lyre has been attributed to Phoebus; for this reason the ancients believed Harmonia ought to be regarded as the daughter of Jove and Electra, whom the whole choir of heaven is said to have lauded in song when she had been given Cadmus in marriage.

But supposing no one on earth had ever heard this symphony of the stars, does it therefore follow that all has been silent beyond the circle of the moon, and lulled to sleep by the benumbing silence? Nay rather, let us blame our feeble ears which are not able, or are not worthy, to overhear the songs and such sweet tones. But this melody of the sky is not really unheard; for who, O Aristotle, would have conceived of your meteors as dancing in the mid-region of the air, except that, when they hear the singing heavens clearly on account of their nearness, they cannot restrain themselves from performing a choral dance?

But Pythagoras alone of mortals is said to have heard this song; unless that good man was both some deity and native of the sky, who perchance by direction of the gods had descended for the purpose of instructing the minds of men with holy knowledge and of calling upon them to improve. Certainly he was a man who combined in himself the whole gamut of virtues and who was worthy to converse with the very gods like unto himself and to enjoy the company of the celestials. Therefore, I do not wonder that the gods, loving him very much, permitted him to take part in the most secret mysteries of Nature.

Moreover, the boldness of the thieving Prometheus seems to be the reason why we hear so little this harmony, a deed which brought upon humanity so many ills and likewise took away this happiness from us, which we shall never be permitted to enjoy so long as we remain brutish and overwhelmed by wicked animal desires[38]; for how can those be susceptible of that heavenly sound whose souls, as Persius says, are bent toward the earth and absolutely devoid of celestial matters? But if we possessed hearts so pure, so spotless, so snowy, as once upon a time Pythagoras had, then indeed would our ears be made to resound and to be completely filled with that most delicious music of the revolving stars; and then all things would return immediately as it were to that golden age; then, at length, freed from miseries we should spend our time in peace, blessed and envied even by the gods.[39]

On the Purpose of Music

IN A SONNET Milton seems to argue for an inherent value in music, when he suggests that for those who understand music, hearing it often is not unwise.

> Whence we may rise
> To hear the Lute well touched, or artful voice
> Warble immortal Notes and Tuscan Ayre?
> He who of those delights can judge, And spare
> To interpose them oft, is not unwise.[40]

[38] In "An Apology," in Ibid., III, 306, Milton also states that "celestial music is inaudible to the unchaste."

[39] "On the Music of the Spheres," in Ibid., XII, 149ff.

[40] "Sonnet XX," in Ibid., I, 67.

Milton often, especially in the pastoral settings, has his characters listen to music purely for pleasure, for example the reference "with jocond Music charm his ear" in "Paradise Lost,"[41] or in the pastoral figure in "Il Penseroso" who awakes to sweet music.

[41] "Paradise Lost," in I, 787, Ibid., II, 36.

> And as I wake, sweet musick breath
> Above, about, or underneath,
> Sent by some spirit to mortals good,
> Or the unseen Genius of the Wood.[42]

[42] "Il Penseroso," in Ibid., I, 45.

A more extended example is found in another poem, "The Hymn":

> When such musick sweet
> Their hearts and ears did greet,
> As never was by mortal finger struck,
> Divinely-warbled voice
> Answering the stringed noise,
> As all their souls in blissfull rapture took ...
> Such Musick (as 'tis said)
> Before was never made ...
>
> She knew such harmony alone
> Could hold all Heaven and Earth in happier union.[43]

[43] "The Hymn," in Ibid., I, 5.

The most traditional purpose for music given in early literature is to soothe the listener, as we find in a lovely pastoral scene in Milton's "Mask."

> I sat me down to watch upon a bank
> With Ivy canopied, and interwove
> With flaunting Honeysuckle, and began
> Wrapt in a pleasing fit of melancholy
> To mediate upon my rural minstrelsie,
> Till fancy had her fill ...[44]
> Ever against eating Cares,
> Lap me in soft *Lydian* Aires ...
> Untwisting all the chains that tie
> The hidden soul of harmony ...[45]

[44] "A Mask," in Ibid., I, 105.

[45] "L'Allegro," in Ibid., I, 39.

In the poem, "Mansus," Milton describes Apollo: "to the strains of the lute, he soothed with his voice the hard labors of his exile."[46] A rather extraordinary reference to listening

[46] "Mansus," in Ibid., I, 293.

to music is found in "Paradise Regained," when Jesus says to Satan that "I would delight my private hours with music or with poem" for the purpose of solace, provided it is in the Hebrew language.[47]

[47] "Paradise Regained," IV, 331, in Ibid., II, 471.

The most important purpose of music is to express feeling and the emotionally expressive nature of music is vividly discussed by Milton in a poem dedicated to his father. The portion below begins with reference to the ancient Rhapsodists who sang epic poetry and concludes with a very interesting tribute to the close relationship of music and oratory, skills which Milton apparently admired in his father. One can indeed find a close relationship between music and oratory in the sense that it is the right hemisphere of the brain which provides the emotional coloring which determines meaning for both. Milton, unaware of modern discoveries in brain function, instinctively uses "music" as a metaphor for this right hemisphere emotional input.

> Songs, were wont, in olden days, to adorn the rich feasts of kings, when luxury, and the limitless abyss of the bottomless gullet were yet unknown, and the banquet tables foamed only with modest wines. In those days, the bard, seated in accord with custom at the holiday feast, his unshorn locks bound with leaves from the oak-tree, used to sing of the achievements of heroes, exploits worthy of imitation, and the foundations, laid broad and wide, of the world, and of gods creeping, and of acorns that formed food for gods, and of the lightning-bolt not yet sought from Aetna's grot. In brief, what pleasure will there be in music well attuned if it is empty of voice, empty of words and of their meanings, and of numbers that talk? Such strains befit the woodland choirs, not Orpheus, who by his songs, not by his lyre, and by his singing compelled to tears the shades that were done with life: it is from his *song* that he has these praises.
>
> Persist not, I pray you, to hold cheap the holy Muses, nor think them idle, poor, for through their bounty you yourself skillfully compose a thousand strains to measures fit, and, since you have been trained to vary your tuneful voice by a thousand modulations, you would of right be heir of Arion's fame. Wherein is it strange if it has fallen to your lot to sire me, a poet, if we, knit so closely together by dear ties of blood, should pursue arts of one blood, and kindred studies?[48]

[48] "Ad Patrem," in Ibid., I, 274ff.

Another tribute to the expressive power of music is found in a sonnet:

> When, beautiful, thou speakest, or, in mood of happiness, sing in such guise that the hardest and wildest oak is moved to feeling, one must guard the gateways to ear and eye ...[49]

[49] "Sonnet II," in Ibid., I, 49.

We also find in Milton's work references to the ancient Greek belief that music can change one's character or manners, although he seems to assume some connection with the music of the spheres. In the poem "Arcades," he attributes to music the ability to raise man above disturbing influences.

> Such sweet compulsion doth in musick lie,
> To lull the daughters of Necessity,
> And keep unsteady Nature to her law,
> And the low world in measured motion draw
> After the heavenly tune, which none can hear
> Of human mold with gross unpurged ear ...[50]

[50] "Arcades," in Ibid., I, 74.

In the poem, "To Leonora, as She Sings at Rome," music is referred to as a "Third Intelligence" which comes from Heaven which enters the throat of the singer and "graciously teaches mortal hearts the power to grow accustomed insensibly to sounds immortal."[51] Another poem contains a brief reference to music used for prophesy, "Then sing of secret things that came to pass."[52]

[51] "To Leonora, as She Sings at Rome," in Ibid., I, 229.

[52] "At a Vacation Exercise," in Ibid., I, 20.

Milton frequently mentions art songs in a pastoral setting, in particular in his Masque[53] and in his poem, "Arcades." Another pastoral poem, "Elegia Sexta," includes instrumental art music: "Now the Thracian lyre, too, with its fretted gold, sounds for you, touched softly by an artist hand."[54]

[53] "A Mask," in Ibid., I, 105, lines 546ff.

[54] Lines 43ff.

The presence of the contemplative listener also identifies true art music, as in this example:

> Such as the wise *Demodocus* once told
> In solemn Songs at King *Alcinous* feast,
> While sad *Ulisses* soul and all the rest
> Are held with his melodious harmony
> In willing chains and sweet captivity.[55]

[55] "At a Vacation Exercise," in Ibid., I, 20.

And also in "Paradise Lost":

Their Song was partial, but the harmony
(What could it less when Spirits immortal sing?)
Suspended Hell, and took with ravishment
The thronging audience.[56]

[56] "Paradise Lost," II, 552, in Ibid., II, 57.

Bibliography

1 Music at the Jacobean Court

Ashton, Robert. *James I*. London: Hutchinson.

Dart, Thurston. "The Repertory of the Royal Wind Music." *The Galpin Society Journal,* 11 (May, 1958): 70–77.

Donnington, Robert. *The Interpretation of Early Music*. New York, 1964.

Dugdale, Gilbert. *The Time Triumphant*. London, 1604.

Hibbert, Christopher. *Charles I*. New York: Harper.

Jones, Paul. *The Household of a Tudor Nobleman*. Urbana, 1918.

Lafontaine, Henry. *The King's Music*. New York, 1973.

Lord Chamberlains Accounts, vol. 738, p. 75, for January 10, 1629. London.

Nichols, John. *The Progresses of Queen Elizabeth*. London, 1805.

Playford, John. *An Introduction to the Skill of Music* [1674]. Ridgewood: Gregg Press, 1966.

Shedlock, J. S. *Coronation Music*. London: Royal Music Society, 28th Session.

Walls, Peter. "London, 1603–49," in *The Early Baroque Era*. Englewood Cliffs: Prentice Hall, 1994.

Wilson, John. *Roger North on Music*. London: Novello, 1959.

Woodfill, Walter. *Musicians in English Society*. Princeton, 1953.

2 Music in the Masque

Beaumont and Fletcher. *Complete Plays*. Cambridge: University Press, 1912.

Bullen, A. H. *The Works of John Marston*. London: Nimmo, 1887.

Calendar of State Papers and Manuscripts existing in the Archives of Venice, 1617–1619.

Dart, Thurston. "The Repertory of the Royal Wind Music." *The Galpin Society Journal*, 11 (May, 1958): 70–77.

The Description of a Maske, presented before the kinges majestie at Whitehall ... London, 1607.

Durant, Will. *The Age of Reason Begins*. New York: Simon and Schuster, 1961.

Evans, Willa. *Ben Jonson and Elizabethan Music*. New York, 1965.

Grosart. *The Non-Dramatic Works of Thomas Dekker*. New York, Russell & Russell, 1963.

Heywood, Thomas. *The Dramatic Works of Thomas Heywood*. New York: Russell & Russell, 1964.

Holaday, Allan. *The Plays of George Chapman; the Comedies*. Urbana: University of Illinois Press, 1970.

Nichols, *The Progresses of King James The First*. London, 1828.

Reese, Gustave. *Music in the Renaissance*. New York, 1959.

Bacon, Francis. *The Works of Francis Bacon*. Edited by James Spedding. Cambridge: Cambridge University Press, 1869.

The Works of Thomas Middleton. New York: AMS Press, 1964.

3 Jacobean Church Music

The Autobiographical Notes of Elias Ashmole. Edited by C. H. Josten. Oxford, 1966.

Dauney, W. *Ancient Scottish Melodies*. Edinburgh, 1838.

Davey, H. *History of English Music*. London, 1921.

Donne, John. *Devotions Upon Emergent Occasion*. Edited by Anthony Raspa. Montreal: McGill-Queen's University Press, 1975.

Holman, Peter. "London: Commonwealth and Restoration." In *The Early Baroque Era*. Englewood Cliffs: Prentice Hall, 1994.

Lafontaine, Henry. *The King's Music*. New York, 1973.

Milton, John. "Church-Government" in *The Works of John Milton*. Edited by Frank Patterson. New York: Columbia University Press, 1931–1938.

Nichols, *The Progresses of King James The First*. London, 1828.

Ornsby, G., ed. "The Correspondence of John Cosin, D. D." In *Surtee Society*. London, 1869.

Parrott, Andrew. "Grett and Solompne Singing." *Early Music* 6, no. 2 (April, 1978): 182–187.

Peacham, H. *The Compleat Gentleman*. 1622.

Smart, Peter. *A Catalogue of Superstitious Innovations*. London, 1642.

———. *A Sermon Preached in the Cathedrall Church of Durham, July 7, 1628*. London, 1640.

Strype, J. *Annals of the Reformation*. London, 1709.

Walls, Peter. "London, 1603–49." In *The Early Baroque Era*. Englewood Cliffs: Prentice Hall, 1994.

Woodfill, Walter. *Musicians in English Society*. Princeton, 1953.

4 Music in Jacobean Society

Carew, Thomas. *The Poems of Thomas Carew*. Edited by Rhodes Dunlap. Oxford: Clarendon Press, 1964.

Crashaw, Richard. *The Complete Poetry of Richard Crashaw*. Edited by George Williams. New York: New York University Press, 1972.

Herbert, George. *The Poems of George Herbert*. Edited by Ernest Rhys. London: Walter Scott, 1885.

Heywood, Thomas. *The Dramatic Works of Thomas Heywood*. New York: Russell & Russell, 1964.

Jonson, Ben. *The Complete Poetry of Ben Jonson*. Edited by William Hunter. New York: Norton, 1963.

James I. *New Poems of James I*. Edited by Allan Westcott. New York: AMS Press, 1966.

North, Roger. *The Musicall Gramarian*. Oxford: Oxford University Press, 1925.

Suckling, Sir John. *The Works of Sir John Suckling.* Edited by Hamilton Thompson. New York: Russell & Russell, 1964.
Wilson, John. *Roger North on Music.* London: Novello, 1959.
Wither, George. *Works of George Wither.* New York: Franklin, 1967.

5 Music in the Jacobean Theater

Beaumont, Francis (1584–1616) and John Fletcher (1579–1625). *The Bloody Brother.*
———. *Bonduca.*
———. *The Burning Pesstle.*
———. *The Captain.*
———. *The Coronation.*
———. *The Chances.*
———. *Cupid's Revenge.*
———. *The Double Marriage.*
———. *The Elder Brother.*
———. *The Faithful Shepherdess.*
———. *The False One.*
———. *The Humourous Lieutenant.*
———. *A King, and No King.*
———. *The Knight of the Burning Pestle.*
———. *The Knight of Malta.*
———. *The Little French Lawyer.*
———. *The Lovers Progress.*
———. *The Loyal Subject.*
———. *The Mad Lover.*
———. *The Maid in the Mill.*
———. *The Maids Tragedy.*
———. *Monsieur Thomas.*
———. *The Pilgrim.*
———. *The Prophetess.*
———. *The Queen of Corinth.*
———. *The Sea-Voyage.*
———. *The Spanish Curate.*
———. *Thierry and Theodoret.*
———. *The Tragedy of Valentiniam.*
———. *The Two Noble Kinsmen.*

———. *Wit at Several Weapons.*
———. *Women Pleased.*
Chapman, George (1559-1634). *Alphonsus Emperor of Germany.*
———. *The Blind Beggar.*
———. *Revenge for Honor.*
———. *The Tragedy of Caesar and Pompey.*
———. *The Widow's Tears.*
Dekker, Thomas (1572–1632). *Old Fortunatus.*
———. *The Honest Whore.*
———. *If This be not a Good Play.*
———. *Lust's Dominion.*
———. *The Noble Spanish Soldier.*
———. *Patient Grissil.*
———. *The Roaring Girle.*
———. *Satiromastix.*
———. *The Shoemaker's Holiday.*
———. *Sir Thomas Wyatt.*
———. *The Virgin Martyr.*
———. *The Welsh Embassador.*
———. *Westward Ho.*
———. *The Whore of Babylon.*
———. *The Wonder of a Kingdom.*
Jonson, Ben (1572–1637). *Cynthia's Revels.*
———. *The Devil is an Ass.*
———. *Poetaster.*
———. *The Silent Woman.*
Heywood, Thomas (1575–1641). *The English Traveller.*
———. *Fortune by Land and Sea.*
———. *The foure Prentises of London.*
———. *The Golden Age.*
———. *If you know not me, you know no body.*
———. *The Iron Age.*
———. *King Edward the fourth.*
———. *Loves Mistris.*
———. *A Maiden-head well lost.*
———. *The Rape of Lucrece.*
———. *The Witches of Lancashire.*
———. *A Woman Kilde wth Kindnesse.*

Marston, John (1576–1634). *Antonio and Mellida.*
———. *The Dutch Courtezan.*
———. *The Fawn.*
———. *The Insatiate Countess.*
———. *The Malcontent.*
———. *The Tragedy of Sophonisba.*
———. *What You Will.*
Middleton, Thomas (1580–1637). *Blurt, Master-Constable.*
———. *A Chaste Maid in Cheapside.*
———. *A Mad World, my Masters.*
———. *Mayor of Queenborough.*
———. *More Dissemblers Besides Women.*
———. *The Spanish Gipsy.*
———. *The Witch.*
Shirley, James (1596–1666). *The Cardinal.*
Tourneur, Cyril (1575–1626). *The Atheist's Tragedy.*
———. *The Revenger's Trasgedy.*
Webster, John (1580–1634). *The Dutchesse of Malfy.*

6 Music in Jacobean Poetry

Carew, Thomas. *The Poems of Thomas Carew.* Edited by Rhodes Dunlap. Oxford: Clarendon Press.
Crashaw, Richard. *The Complete Poetry of Richard Crashaw.* Edited by George Williams. New York: New York University Press, 1972.
Donne, John. *The Complete Poetry of John Donne.* New York: New York University Press, 1968.
Herbert, George. *The Poems of George Herbert.* Edited by Ernest Rhys. London: Walter Scott, 1885.
Herrick, Robert. *The Poetical Works of Robert Herrick.* Edited by L. C. Martin. Oxford: Clarendon Press, 1963.
Jonson, Ben. *The Complete Poetry of Ben Jonson.* Edited by William Hunter. New York: Norton, 1963.
Lovelace, Richard. *The Poems of Richard Lovelace.* Edited by C. H. Wilkinson. Oxford: Clarendon Press, 1930.
Marvell, Andrew. *The Complete Works of Andrew Marvell.* New York: AMS Press, 1966.

Vaughan, Henry. *The Works of Henry Vaughan*. Edited by L. C. Martin. Oxford: At the Clarendon Press, 1957.

Wither, George. *Works of George Wither*. New York: Franklin, 1967.

7 Music in Jacobean Prose

Browne, Sir Thomas. *Sir Thomas Browne's Works*. Edited by Simon Wilkin. London: Pickering, 1836.

The "Conceited Newes" of Sir Thomas Overbury and His Friends. Edited by James Savage. Gainesville: Scholars' Facsimiles, 1968.

Earle, John. *Microcosmography* [1628]. St. Clair Shores: Scholarly Press, 1971.

Fuller, Thomas. *The Holy State and the Profance State* [1642]. Edited by Maximilian Walten. New York: AMS Press, 1966.

Grosart. *The Non-Dramatic Works of Thomas Dekker*. New York, Russell & Russell, 1963.

Walton, Izaak. *The Compleat Angler*. London: Oxford University Press, 1935.

8 Entertainment Music in Baroque England

Bullen, A. H. *The Works of John Marston*. London: Nimmo, 1887.

Butler, Samuel. *Characters*.

Defoe, Daniel. *A Journal of the Plague Year*. Garden City: Doubleday.

Donne, John. *Selected Prose*. Edited by Helen Gardner. Oxford: Clarendon Press, 1967.

Dekker, Thomas. *The Dramatic Works of Thomas Dekker*. Edited by Fredson Bowers. Cambridge: University Press, 1955.

Earle, John. *Microcosmography* [1628]. St. Clair Shores: Scholarly Press, 1971.

Gay, John. *The Works of John Gay*. London: Edward Jeffery, 1745.

Gray, Thomas. *Correspondence of Thomas Gray*. Oxford, Clarendon Press, 1971.

Grosart. *The Non-Dramatic Works of Thomas Dekker*. New York, Russell & Russell, 1963.
Heywood, Thomas. *The Dramatic Works of Thomas Heywood*. New York: Russell & Russell, 1964.
Middleton, Thomas. *The Works of Thomas Middleton*. New York: AMS Press, 1964.
Pepys, Samuel. *The Pepys Ballads*. Cambridge: Harvard University Press, 1929.
Shenstone, William. *Letters of William Shenstone*. Minneapolis: University of Minnesota Press, 1939.
———. *Men and Manners*. Boston: Houghton Mifflin, 1927.
The Spectator.
Wither, George. *Works of George Wither*. New York: Franklin, 1967.
Wycherley, William. *The Complete Works of William Wycherley*. New York: Russell & Russell, 1964.

9 Military Music of the English Baroque

Barry, Gerat. *A Discourse of Military Discipline*. Brussels, 1634.
Bunyan, John. *The Works of John Bunyan*. Edited by George Offor. London: Blackie and Son, 1853.
Croft-Murray, Edward. "The Wind-Band in England." In *Music & Civilisation*. London, 1980.
Digges, Thomas. *An Arithmetical Warlike Treatise*. London, 1590.
Dryden, John. *The Works of John Dryden*. Edited by Walter Scott. London: William Miller, 1808.
Du Praissac. *The Art of Warre*. Cambridge, 1639.
Elton, Richard. *The Compleat Body of the Art Military*. London, 1650.
Farmer, Henry. *Military Music*. London, 1912.
———. *Handel's Kettledrums*. London, 1965.
Grove, George, ed. *Dictionary of Music*. 1980.
Markham. *Five Decades of Epistles of Warre*. 1622.
McGrady, Richard. "The Court Trumpeters of Charles I and Charles II." *The Music Review*, 1974.
Panoff, Peter. *Militarmusik*. Berlin, 1944.
Pepys, Samuel. *Diary*.

Prior, Matthew. *The Literary Works of Matthew Prior*. Oxford: Clarendon, 1959.
Springell, Francis. *Connoisseur & Diplomat*. London, 1936.
Walpole. *Catalogue of Royal and Noble Authors*.
Young, Edward. *Edward Young: The Complete Works*. Hildesheim: Olms, 1968.

10 *Views by English Musicians of the Baroque*

Avison, Charles. *An Essay on Musical Expression* [London, 1753]. New York: Broude Reprint, 1967.
Butler, Charles. *The Principles of Musik in Singing and Setting* [1636]. New York: Da Capo Press, 1970.
Donnington, Robert. *The Interpretation of Early Music*. New York, 1964.
Mace, Thomas. *Musick's Monument* [1676]. Paris: Editions du Centre National de la Recherche Scientifique, 1966.
Playford, John. *An Introduction to the Skill of Music* [1674]. Ridgewood: Gregg Press, 1966.
Simpson, Christopher. *A Compendium of Practical Music*, Second Edition of 1667. Oxford: Blackwell, 1970.
———. *Division-Violist* [1654]. London: Curwen, 1965.
Walls, Peter. "London, 1603–49." In *The Early Baroque Era*. Englewood Cliffs: Prentice Hall, 1994.

11 *Contemporary Views on Performance Practice*

Avison, Charles. *An Essay on Musical Expression* [London, 1753]. New York: Broude Reprint, 1967.
Burney, Charles. *General History of Music* [1776]. London, 1935.
Crashaw, Richard. *The Complete Poetry of Richard Crashaw*. Edited by George Williams. New York: New York University Press, 1972.
Donnington, Robert. *The Interpretation of Early Music*. New York, 1964.
Hawkins, John. *A General History of the Science and Practice of Music* [1776]. New York: Dover Reprint, 1963.

Herbert, George. *The Poems of George Herbert*. Edited by Ernest Rhys. London: Walter Scott, 1885.

Herrick, Robert. *The Poetical Works of Robert Herrick*. Oxford: Clarendon Press, 1963.

Milton, John. *The Works of John Milton*. Edited by Frank Patterson. New York: Columbia University Press, 1931–1938.

North, Roger. *Memoirs of Music*. Edited by Edward Rimbault. London: Bell, 1846.

Playford, John. *An Introduction to the Skill of Music* [1674]. Ridgewood: Gregg Press, 1966.

Wilson, John. *Roger North on Music*. London: Novello, 1959.

The Works of Francis Bacon (Cambridge: Cambridge University Press, 1869.

12 Jacobean Philosophers on Music

Bunyan, John. *The Works of John Bunyan*. Edited by George Offort. London: Blackie and Son, 1853.

Burton, Robert. *The Anatomy of Melancholy*. Edited by Floyd Dell. New York: Tudor Publishing Company, 1938.

Donne, John. *Selected Prose*. Edited by Helen Gardner. Oxford: Clarendon Press, 1967.

———. *Five Sermons*. Menston: Scolar Press, 1970.

Donnington, Robert. *The Interpretation of Early Music*. New York, 1964.

Hall, Joseph. *The Works of Joseph Hall, D. D.* Edited by Philip Wynter. New York: AMS Press, 1969.

Harvey, William. *Lectures on the Whole of Anatomy*. Berkeley: University of California Press, 1961.

13 North on Music

Wilson, John. *Roger North on Music*. London: Novello, 1959.

14 Bacon on Music

Bacon, Francis. *The Works of Francis Bacon.* Edited by James Spedding. Cambridge: Cambridge University Press, 1869.

Durant, Will. *The Age of Reason Begins.* New York: Simon and Schuster, 1961.

15 Milton on Music

Milton, John. *The Works of John Milton.* Edited by Frank Patterson. New York: Columbia University Press, 1931-1938.

About the Author

Dr. David Whitwell is a graduate ("with distinction") of the University of Michigan and the Catholic University of America, Washington DC (PhD, Musicology, Distinguished Alumni Award, 2000) and has studied conducting with Eugene Ormandy and at the Akademie für Musik, Vienna. Prior to coming to Northridge, Dr. Whitwell participated in concerts throughout the United States and Asia as Associate First Horn in the USAF Band and Orchestra in Washington DC, and in recitals throughout South America in cooperation with the United States State Department.

At the California State University, Northridge, which is in Los Angeles, Dr. Whitwell developed the CSUN Wind Ensemble into an ensemble of international reputation, with international tours to Europe in 1981 and 1989 and to Japan in 1984. The CSUN Wind Ensemble has made professional studio recordings for BBC (London), the Köln Westdeutscher Rundfunk (Germany), NOS National Radio (The Netherlands), Zürich Radio (Switzerland), the Television Broadcasting System (Japan) as well as for the United States State Department for broadcast on its "Voice of America" program. The CSUN Wind Ensemble's recording with the Mirecourt Trio in 1982 was named the "Record of the Year" by *The Village Voice*. Composers who have guest conducted Whitwell's ensembles include Aaron Copland, Ernest Krenek, Alan Hovhaness, Morton Gould, Karel Husa, Frank Erickson and Vaclav Nelhybel.

Dr. Whitwell has been a guest professor in 100 different universities and conservatories throughout the United States and in 23 foreign countries (most recently in China, in an elite school housed in the Forbidden City). Guest conducting experiences have included the Philadelphia Orchestra, Seattle Symphony Orchestra, the Czech Radio Orchestras of Brno and Bratislava, The National Youth Orchestra of Israel, as well as resident wind ensembles in Russia, Israel, Austria, Switzerland, Germany, England, Wales, The Netherlands, Portugal, Peru, Korea, Japan, Taiwan, Canada and the United States.

He is a past president of the College Band Directors National Association, a member of the Prasidium of the International Society for the Promotion of Band Music, and was a member of the founding board of directors of the World Association for Symphonic Bands and Ensembles (WASBE). In 1964 he was made an honorary life member of Kappa Kappa Psi, a national professional music fraternity. In September, 2001, he was a delegate to the UNESCO Conference on Global Music in Tokyo. He has been knighted by sovereign organizations in France, Portugal and Scotland and has been awarded the gold medal of Kerkrade, The Netherlands, and the silver medal of Wangen, Germany, the highest honor given wind conductors in the United States, the medal of the Academy of Wind and Percussion Arts (National Band Association) and the highest honor given wind conductors in Austria, the gold medal of the Austrian Band Association. He is a member of the Hall of Fame of the California Music Educators Association.

Dr. Whitwell's publications include more than 127 articles on wind literature including publications in *Music and Letters* (London), the *London Musical Times*, the *Mozart-Jahrbuch* (Salzburg), and 50 books, among which is his 13-volume *History and Literature of the Wind Band and Wind Ensemble* and an 8-volume series on *Aesthetics in Music*. In addition to numerous modern editions of early wind band music his original compositions include five symphonies.

David Whitwell was named as one of six men who have determined the course of American bands during the second half of the twentieth century, in the definitive history, *The Twentieth Century American Wind Band* (Meredith Music). A doctoral dissertation by German Gonzales (2007, Arizona State University) is dedicated to the life and conducting career of David Whitwell through the year 1977. David Whitwell is one of nine men described by Paula A. Crider in *The Conductor's Legacy* (Chicago: GIA, 2010) as "the legendary conductors" of the twentieth century.

> "I can't imagine the 2nd half of the 20th century—without David Whitwell and what he has given to all of the rest of us."
> Frederick Fennell (1993)

About the Editor

CRAIG DABELSTEIN began studying the piano at age seven and took up the saxophone at age twelve. Mr Dabelstein has Bachelor of Arts (Music) and Bachelor of Music degrees from the Queensland Conservatorium of Music and a Graduate Diploma of Learning and Teaching and a Graduate Certificate in Editing and Publishing from the University of Southern Queensland. He has held the principal saxophone chairs in the Australian Wind Orchestra and has been an augmenting member of the Queensland Philharmonic and Symphony Orchestras. He was a member of the Queensland Saxophone Quartet and has previously been a saxophone teacher at the Queensland Conservatorium of Music. He is a regular conductor of the Queensland Wind Orchestra and has been a research associate for the *Teaching Music Through Performance in Band* series of books. He is the editor of more than forty books by Dr. David Whitwell including *A Concise History of the Wind Band, Foundations of Music Education, Music Education of the Future, The Sousa Oral History Project, Wagner on Bands, Berlioz on Bands, The Art of Musical Conducting, Aesthetics of Music* (8 volumes) and *The History and Literature of the Wind Band and Wind Ensemble* (13 volumes). He currently teaches saxophone and clarinet, and conducts bands at St Joseph's College, Gregory Terrace.

Books by David Whitwell

- The Sousa Oral History Project
- The Art of Musical Conducting
- The Longy Club: 1900–1917
- La Téléphonie and the Universal Musical Language
- Extraordinary Women
- A Concise History of the Wind Band
- Essays on the Modern Wind Band
- Essays on Performance Practice
- A New History of Wind Music
- The College and University Band
- The Early Symphonies of Mozart
- Band Music of the French Revolution
- A Conductor's Diary

On Philosophy and Performance Practice

- Essays on Music of the German Baroque: Philosophy and Performance Practice
- Essays on Music of the French Baroque: Philosophy and Performance Practice
- Essays on Italian and Spanish Music of the Baroque: Philosophy and Performance Practice
- Philosophy and Performance Practice of Music during Jacobean England
- Philosophy and Performance Practice of Music during Restoration England

On Composers

- Wagner on Bands
- Berlioz on Bands
- Chopin: A Self-Portrait
- Liszt: A Self-Portrait
- Schumann: A Self-Portrait in His Own Words
- Mendelssohn: A Self-Portrait in His Own Words

On Education

- Philosophic Foundations of Education
- Foundations of Music Education
- Music Education of the Future

Aesthetics of Music

- Aesthetics of Music in Ancient Civilizations
- Aesthetics of Music in the Middle Ages
- Aesthetics of Music in the Early Renaissance
- Aesthetics of Music in Sixteenth-Century Italy, France and Spain
- Aesthetics of Music in Sixteenth-Century Germany, the Low Countries and England
- Aesthetics of Baroque Music in Italy, Spain, the German-Speaking Countries and the Low Countries
- Aesthetics of Baroque Music in France
- Aesthetics of Baroque Music in England

The History and Literature of the Wind Band and Wind Ensemble Series

- Volume 1 The Wind Band and Wind Ensemble Before 1500
- Volume 2 The Renaissance Wind Band and Wind Ensemble
- Volume 3 The Baroque Wind Band and Wind Ensemble
- Volume 4 The Wind Band and Wind Ensemble of the Classical Period (1750–1800)
- Volume 5 The Nineteenth-Century Wind Band and Wind Ensemble
- Volume 6 A Catalog of Multi-Part Repertoire for Wind Instruments or for Undesignated Instrumentation before 1600
- Volume 7 Baroque Wind Band and Wind Ensemble Repertoire
- Volume 8 Classical Period Wind Band and Wind Ensemble Repertoire
- Volume 9 Nineteenth-Century Wind Band and Wind Ensemble Repertoire
- Volume 10 A Supplementary Catalog of Wind Band and Wind Ensemble Repertoire
- Volume 11 A Catalog of Wind Repertoire before the Twentieth Century for One to Five Players
- Volume 12 A Second Supplementary Catalog of Early Wind Band and Wind Ensemble Repertoire
- Volume 13 Name Index, Volumes 1–12, The History and Literature of the Wind Band and Wind Ensemble

Ancient Voices

- Ancient Views on Music and Religion
- Ancient Views on the Natural World
- Ancient Views on What Is Music
- Contemporary Descriptions of Early Musicians
- Early Views of Music and Ethics
- Early Thoughts on Performance Practice
- Music Performance in Ancient Societies

Renaissance Voices

- Essays on Renaissance Philosophies of Music
- Renaissance Men on Music

www.whitwellbooks.com

www.ingramcontent.com/pod-product-compliance
Lightning Source LLC
Chambersburg PA
CBHW080549230426
43663CB00015B/2768